Making your own Liqueurs

Joyce van Doorn

Making your own Liqueurs

Recipes for making fruits in alcohol, ratafias, liqueurs from herbs and flowers, bitters, elixirs, and love-potions

Prism Press

Published in the U.K. in 1980 by
PRISM PRESS
Sherborne, Dorset

and in the U.S.A. by
PRISM PRESS
P.O. Box 778
San Leandro
California, 94577

Originally published in Holland by Uitgeverij Bert Bakker 1977

Translated by First Edition and
published by agreement with Writers House Inc.,
21 West 26 Street, New York 10010

© 1977 Joyce van Doorn
© 1980 English translation Prism Press
© 1980 Liqueurs from English Wines Brian Leverett

ISBN 0 907061 03 6 (Hardback)
ISBN 0 907061 04 4 (Paperback)

Distributed in the U.S.A. by Interbook Inc.,
861 Lawrence Drive, Newbury Park, California 91320

Distributed in Australia by Doubleday Australia Pty Ltd.,
14 Mars Road, Lane Cove, N.S.W. 2066

Distributed in New Zealand by Roulston Greene,
P.O. Box 33-850, Takapuna, Auckland 9

Distributed in South Africa by Trade Winds Press (Pty) Ltd.,
P.O. Box 20194 Durban North 4016

Contents

Introduction

The word 'liqueur' is associated with luxury, refinement, poetry, feelings of satisfaction, and intimacy. A liqueur is a worthy conclusion to a fine meal enjoyed with good company in a peaceful atmosphere. Apricot brandy, plums in brandy, curaçao, or parfait d'amour with a cup of coffee; there is a drink to suit every taste.

In this book you will find a great deal about liqueurs: a bit of history, a little about distilling, spices and drinks, a few anecdotes, and last but not least simple recipes for making your own liqueurs. Making liqueurs is very rewarding work and not too time-consuming, and you get more lasting pleasure from the result than you would from the preparation of a single meal. Someone once said about liqueur making that 'it elicits inventiveness, imagination and creativity.'

You don't need complicated equipment, just a set of scales, glassware, a filter and the following ingredients:

herbs and spices to give an exotic touch, flowers and fruits to remind you of summer, sugar to make life sweeter and alcohol to evoke or strengthen that lovely feeling of euphoria.

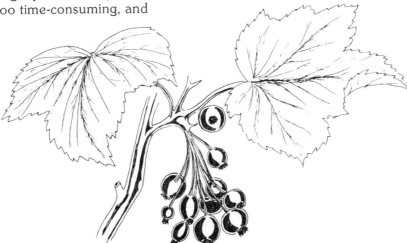

What is a Liqueur?

A liqueur may be defined as a sweetish alcoholic drink flavoured with flowers, fruits, herbs and/or spices, and with an alcohol level of at least 22%. Nowadays, this level usually lies around 35%. The same sort of drink with an alcohol level lower than 22% is called liqueur wine. The following drinks are classified as liqueurs:

Ratafia—for a long time the name given to liqueurs prepared from fruit juices. This term is sometimes used for liqueurs made from flowers and for certain others that are flavoured by letting the ingredients stand rather than by distillation. In this book ratafia refers only to liqueurs made from fruits.

Bitter—a liqueur that owes its typical taste and name to certain bitter spices. A bitter can be sweetened or unsweetened and is drunk most often as an aperitif, in contrast to other liqueurs which are drunk mainly after meals or in the evening.

Elixir—a drink which is said to improve health or life expectancy. Although, strictly speaking, unsweetened elixirs do not qualify as liqueurs, I have included them in this book because they are so closely related. The same goes for other unsweetened drinks which can be found in this book.

Fruits in alcohol, 'flower' liqueurs, 'herb' liqueurs, medicinal liqueurs and love-potions speak for themselves.

For special occasions many concoctions have been dedicated to famous people or created for them just like food dishes: the Liqueur of the Prince of Orange, Eau de la Reine d'Hongrie, Eau de la Reine Isabelle, Eau de la Saltane Zoraide and the rossolis du Roy.

Organisations would sometimes give instructions for the concoction of their own liqueurs. This is how Bols 'freemasons liqueur' originated at the centenary of the Dutch Lodge in 1834 (King William I of Holland joined at that time). Other examples are hunter's liqueur, soldier's liqueur and the *jägermeister*. Women in the lives of the makers were immortalised through names given to liqueurs: Eau de la belle Agathe, Eau de la charmante Clementine, Eau de la gentile Jeanette, to name just a few.

Liqueurs used to be stronger and spicier; the alcoholic strength was around 50% just like gin and brandy. Our ancestors did not flinch at such strong liquor and drank more rather than less of it.

Brandy is lead in the morning, silver at midday and gold in the evening.

German saying.

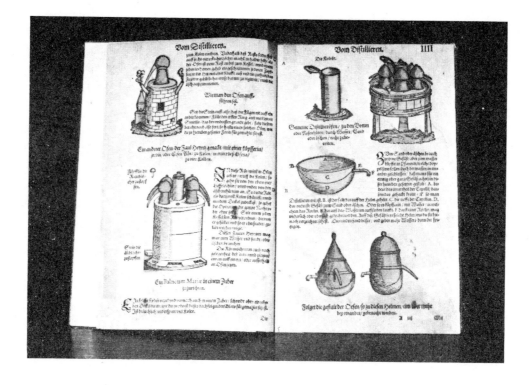

The History of Liqueurs

Origin

The history of liqueurs began with alcohol in the form of wine. The fermentation process, which converts grape juice into wine, must be very old; probably it was known more than two thousand years ago.

An old Persian legend tells of how a woman discovered wine: One day, when old King Jamshid opened a jar in which his grapes were kept, he found a strong-smelling purple liquid. He closed the jar again and had it stored away in his cellars, labelled 'poison'. Later, one of his courtesans, feeling badly neglected and weary of her lonely existence, came across the jar and decided to take her own life. She drank from the jar, fell asleep and lo and behold! she awoke with a feeling of lightheartedness. Joyfully she rushed to the King and told him of her discovery. From that day on many jars of grapes were allowed to ferment and the precious liquid was reserved for royal guests.

From wine to spirits is a big step: wine was the discovery of a natural process, distilled alcohol is the result of science and technology.

Therefore one might expect that the name of the inventor would have survived to this day. Nothing could be further from the truth. Even today, no one knows exactly which civilisation discovered the distillation process. And although archaeologists are revealing more and more secrets of the past, the opinions of scholars are still divided on this point. In turn the following have been suggested as the first distillers: the ancient Egyptians, the Greeks, the scholars of the Alexandrian School, the Arabs and the Italians.

The Egyptians An essay about the distillation process by the Greek-Egyptian philosopher Zozimos led several scholars to conclude that the Egyptians were familiar with distilling. This chemist and scholar is cited in manuscripts which can be found in the Bibliothèque Nationale in Paris and in the library of St. Mark's, Venice, which mainly discuss and comment on the work of his predecessors. Zozimos, who lived at the end of the 3rd century, described various sorts of distillation apparatus, including a *tribikos* (a sort of

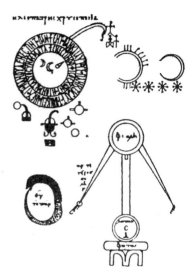

tripod). He said that he had found the drawing of this model in an old temple in Memphis. The story goes that the priests jealously kept the secret of preparation to themselves as well as the resulting drink, an old Egyptian magic potion called 'spirit of wine'. But what it was made from and what effect the magic had are unknown. Furthermore, it is not certain that the translation 'spirit of wine' is correct.

The Greeks According to Alexander of Aphrodisias, Greek physicists like Aristotle (384–322 B.C.) already knew the principles of distilling. In his commentary on the works of Aristotle (albeit 500 years later) he said: 'Sea water can be made drinkable by evaporation, wine and other liquids can be subjected to the same procedure. After they have been reduced to steam they are once again made liquid.'

Herman Schelenz pleaded the Greek case in his history of the distillation apparatus. As a proof of this he advanced the claim of Plinius the Elder (23–79 A.D.) who had observed that 'strong' wine could be ignited. This is difficult to do with ordinary wine, so the Greeks must have been able to increase the alcohol level in some way.

The Chinese There are indications that the Chinese were the first distillers—using rice and barley. Considering the high standard of civilisation these people had attained—they invented many things, such as gunpowder, centuries before us—this does not seem unlikely. However, they are said to have distilled not by heating but by freezing.

This method of distilling (but a very primitive form of it) was described by the explorer Marco Polo and the Franciscan missionary Rubrouck.They came across it in Tartary, and the finding was later confirmed by the Russian archaeologist Pallas who also discovered that the same method was used by Mongolian tribes. It may have been a remnant of Chinese civilisation but could equally well indicate Western influence introduced via China. A distillate made from a mixture of rice and molasses appeared in Ceylon around 800 A.D. The drink, or rather the procedure, is said to have travelled via Japan (*sake*) and Indochina (*choum*) to the Mediterranean coast where the Arabs kept its secret for posterity.

The Scholars of the Alexandrian School

The most likely theory is that Greek-Egyptian chemists of the Alexandrian School developed the distillation process. It seems that this development may be credited to the followers of the famous alchemist Maria, who was Jewish or Egyptian, and who gave her name to the method of cooking in a water bath (*au bain-marie*). Old legends relate that she might have been Moses' sister—a most unlikely story. Maria and her successors, Hermes, Cleopatra and Comarius practised distilling, but not alcohol, only water or powder.

The Arabs Most scholars are agreed on one thing: irrespective of its origin, the distillation process came to Europe via the Arabian alchemists, guardians of Mediterranean civilisation. The Arabic successors of the Alexandrian alchemists distilled mainly scented water (rosewater was especially popular) and powder for cosmetic purposes. This powder has its part in the word 'alcohol'. Alcohol is derived from the Arabic '*Al-koh'l*' the name of a very fine black powder obtained by distillation. Eastern women used this powder as eye make-up and they continue to use it today to blacken the rims of their eyes. In Spain where the Arabic influence, from centuries of Moorish rule, remains noticeable, a certain kind of cow with black rings round its eyes is still called an *alcoholado*. The word alcohol meaning 'the spirit in wine' came into use only a few centuries ago; formerly one spoke of spirit of wine, brandy, or water of life (aqua vitae or eau de vie).

But to return to the Arabs. The first author to report on the distilling of wine was the Arab physician Albucasis. He lived towards the end of the 10th century in Cordoba, Spain, and in voluminous books summarising the work of his predecessors, he discussed the various equipment used for distilling water, vinegar and wine. 'In this way, wine can be distilled by he who cares to distil it' he wrote, but he was not talking about the extraction of alcohol and he did not give any details about the product or the residue.

The Italians A highly-developed wine industry existed from very early times along the Italian coastline. The Italians had good commercial links with the Levant, and in addition the Arabs ruled Sicily during the Byzantine period, until they were expelled by the Normans. As a result of this Arabic influence, Italy produced many alchemists. Taken together, these facts have led many historians, especially the School of Salerno, to suspect that it was here that the first distillation of alcohol took place.

The Middle Ages

Aqua vitae from wine Medieval alchemists, who generally belonged to the nobility or clergy, acquired their wisdom from the Arabs via the Knights of the Cross and the Levanters, who were trading their way across Europe. Generally, these alchemists directed their research towards finding the 'philosopher's stone'—which would convert base metals into precious ones—and the 'water of life' which would prolong life and prevent ageing.

The first manuscript to describe in detail how wine can be distilled was by Marcus Graecus and was called *Liber ignium ad comburendos hostes* (Book of Fire to Burn the Enemy). Nothing is known about the author, but it is surmised that he lived in the 11th or 12th century. He wrote 'Aqua ardente (fire water) can be prepared as follows. Take a full-bodied and old dark wine. To a quart of this wine add 200 grams of well-pulverised sulphur; 1 kilo of wine-stone extracted from a good white wine; 200 grams of unrefined salt. Place all these ingredients in a well-tinned retort. (Modern quantities have been substituted). You will distill into your alambiek

(distillation vessel) aqua ardente, which must be kept in a sealed glass vessel'.

Two very important figures among the alchemists of the Middle Ages were Raymond Lulle (about 1235–1315) and Arnald de Villanova (about 1240–1311). Lulle led a very romantic life. He had a wild youth before his conversion in 1266 when he suddenly heard his calling to drive the Muslims back into the arms of the Mother Church. After many successful attempts he was finally stoned to death by the Arabs.

His achievement lies chiefly in the preparation of highly purified aqua ardente which he named 'quintessence' (fifth essence).

De Villanova was a Catalan doctor who taught at the University of Montpellier. In his essay *Liber de Vinis* he described the

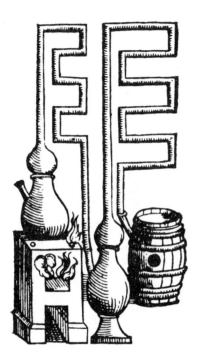

distillation of alcoholic liquids, essences and medicinal wines in a very systematic way. He said about brandy 'We call it aqua vitae and this name is most appropriate since it really is immortal water. It prolongs life, alleviates bad humour, gladdens the heart, and preserves youth.'

De Villanova also added to the medicinal qualities of aqua vitae with officinal herbs. He even sweetened the drink for his patients to make it more palatable!

Soon after the discovery of aqua vitae by the alchemists, brandy drinking became common throughout Europe. It is evident from the *Inventaire des Archives* of Bruges that brandy distilling was a flourishing household industry in the 14th century. Furthermore, a Dutch word for brandy, *bernewijn* has been found on invoices dating from the same period, in Gelderland.

Aqua vitae from grain Although the preparation of brandy from grain is much more complicated than from grapes, it may be assumed that this was also discovered between the 12th and 14th centuries, but very little is known about it. An Irish legend tells us that St. Patrick taught the art of distilling to the Irish, and when the Normans invaded Ireland in the 12th century they found a drink which was possibly distilled from grain. The name of this drink was *uisega beatha*, the Celtic equivalent of aqua vitae, which later became whiskey. Initially the drink was produced by monks for medicinal purposes, but the Irish liked it so much that it became a household industry in the 15th century and since then distilling for personal consumption has been widespread.

Brandy prepared from grain was also known in Germanic countries in the 15th century, but one wonders about its virtues: it was called *Schnapsteufel*, the drink of the Devil, instead of aqua vitae, which continued to be the name used for brandy from wine. It is not known when distilling from grain started in the Netherlands, but considering the large amounts of grain that were stored in ports like Bruges and Antwerp, it would not be surprising to find that the technique was in early use there too. After all, Holland was known as the Granary of Europe, and wine had to be imported in those days.

The Renaissance and Later

In the Renaissance, people at last found time to enjoy the good things in life and to refine them. We owe the creation of liqueurs as a luxury to the Italians, founders of the Renaissance. While the rest of Europe, still shrouded in the darkness of the 13th and 14th centuries, only took drops of aqua vitae as a medicine, the Italians indulged in a sweet, spicy spirituous drink called *liquore*. These high-living Italians brought the drink to Paris in 1332, but it was not until the arrival of Catherine de Medici in 1533 that liqueur drinking started there in earnest. Catherine and her followers introduced all sorts of refinements such as the commedia dell'arte, gourmet cookery, confectionary, ice-cream with liqueur, and many unknown vegetables, fruits and spices. She started an Italian craze at the French court, assisted by her father-in-law, François I. From France the custom of liqueur drinking spread rapidly through Europe and its name was adopted in most other countries. However, it did not become as popular as brandy and remained a real luxury item to be served chiefly after dinner and at parties.

The most famous and popular liqueurs were

Rossoglio de Rossolis, a rose-scented liqueur, and the Populo, a herbal liqueur with musk, aniseed and cinnamon. The Vespetro, a blend of coriander, angelica and aniseed was another old drink, but soon a cellarful of drinks was developed: the Maraschino, made of a small sour cherry from Dalmatia, Eau d'or, Eau de cédrat, Eau éternelle and many ratafias. All these drinks would have been far too sweet for our taste and their alcoholic level was much higher than we are used to.

An old German liqueur from the 15th century was called the *Aqua Vitae Frederici Tertii* (an aqua vitae compound produced and used by Frederick III). The composition was as follows:

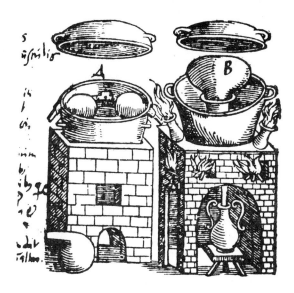

4   pounds of single distilled brandy
3   ounces cinnamon
1   ounce cloves
1½ ounces ginger
1   ounce nutmeg
½   ounce nutmeg flowers
½   ounce zedoary root
2   drachms galangal
½   ounce sage and lavender flowers
1   ounce molasses, violet root, balsam and
1½ ounces white roses
Everything was finely ground and put into a
large retort with:
15-16 pounds sugar
3   ounces dry raisins
6   ounces figs
½   ounce camphor

and 2 pounds of rosewater with an equal amount of chicory water and elderflower water added. (Note that 1 pound = 500 grams and 1 ounce = 100 grams in this recipe). The retort was left in the sun for 20 days, then the liquid was strained and processed further. The knights of that time would drink it before they rode into battle, or use it afterwards as a corpse-reviver!

The golden age of liqueurs began in the 17th century in the time of Ludwig XIV. This King was partial to several ratafias but his favourite was rossolis. He had his own version created, the Rossolis du Roy, which the public was eventually allowed to buy. The Dalmation Maraschino was made to such perfection that its export became very profitable and the Venetian Senate claimed exclusive selling-rights to it. But the ratafias were the most popular because they could easily be made in an ordinary kitchen. Housewives used to exchange recipes, outdoing one another with special drinks, and copying others. In the 18th century, chartreuse became a popular drink. In 1605, the Marshal d'Estrée handed over a long list of 130 mountain plants to the Carthusians of the Vauvert monastery. For years no one knew what to do with this document until a friar-apothecary from the *Grande Chartreuse* monastery deciphered it in 1737, enabling a health elixir, later simply a liqueur, to be prepared: the green chartreuse. The preparation of this drink is still a great secret and only three friars at any one time know its composition. Liqueur distilleries sprung up like mushrooms until well into the 19th century. Although the French Revolution had produced some moderation in eating and drinking habits, dinner was still always concluded with a liqueur. The list of liqueurs that large French restaurants had on their menus in the time of Ludwig 18th and Charles X is incredible:

Marasquin
Gouttes de Malt
Mirobolanty
Cédrat
Eau de vie Dantzich
Huile de Kirchwasser
Eau de vie d'Andaye
Fine Orange
Huile de Rose
Huile de Vanille
Absinthe
Scubac
Crème de Cachou
Elixir de Gaus
Vespetro de chez Tanrade
Gingembre
Barbades
Crème de Cacao à la Vanille
Baume humain
Bois d'Inde
Crème de Créole
Noyau rouge
Alchermes Liquido della Fonderia di S.M.
Novella di Firenze

Brandy and armagnac do not appear on this list, perhaps because these drinks were not unusual enough and therefore considered unworthy of mention.

Liqueurs have always been associated with luxury. In hard times they are one of the first economies. Fashion has a strong influence on people's tastes, and liqueurs enjoyed a brief revival between the two World Wars as an ingredient of cocktails. Similarly, liqueurs are much more popular now than they were 20 years ago, and many forgotten 17th and 18th century drinks are being made again, modified to suit today's consumer trends.

Liqueur Makers

The distillation of alcohol and the preparation of liqueurs was carried out largely in country areas because people there were self-supporting and often had a surplus of raw materials. This went on until it was gradually prohibited by various governments, but there are still many farmers in France and elsewhere who use up their surplus fruit and grain in this way. Usually there is one distillation apparatus hidden away in a shed where the whole neighbourhood take their produce.

In large towns this was more difficult because of the shortage of raw materials and stricter controls.

Even so, in the Renaissance, noblewomen and wealthy merchants' wives would have a stillroom which was an integral part of their quarters. Here they prepared medicinal and cosmetic waters along with drinks for enjoyment.

The less rich could go to the monasteries and apothecaries where one could also get medicine, spices and sugar besides liqueurs. This happened until the advent of Protestantism, which led to the dissolution of 1566. As a result of the monks' expulsion, certain tasks they used to fulfil in daily life were taken over by others and it was not long before the first commercial distilleries came into being. In northern Germany, the Dutchman Ambosien Vermöllen was one of the first to open a liqueur factory, 'der Lachs' in Danzig. France and England did not come by their first commercial ventures until much later because the monasteries were formidable competitors who could produce on a much larger scale.

Not until 1740 did France open the liqueur distillery La Faveur in Montpellier, then in 1749, Giamoco Justerini arrived in England from Italy, and opened a shop which sold a very elaborate drink, *Aqua Mirablis*. This firm still exists, but is now called Justerini & Brooks.

The first liqueur distilleries were very small concerns which depended heavily on local trade and undoubtedly had to take their customers' wishes and tastes into account.

Owing partly to measures taken by the city councils and the government but more especially as a result of social, economic and cultural upheavals, spirit and liqueur distilleries were restricted and centralised.

It appears that liqueur distilling used also to be very important to doctors and apothecaries: the preparation of liqueurs was taught to medical students at Leiden University in the 17th and 18th centuries. The Dutch professor Francis de Boë (Franciscus Silvius), who was very fond of his country's gin, used to teach there.

By the end of the 18th century confectioners had started to practise liqueur distilling as well. Their instruction manuals contained recipes for pastry, liqueurs, chocolate and perfumes. A good example is the book by I.B. Teyras: *the confectioner or the art of confectionary, liqueur distilling and preserving.*

At the beginning of the 20th century confectioners still made liqueurs and essences for their own consumption and one can see exactly how tastes have changed over the years, from the changes in their recipes.

Nowadays liqueurs are only made in factories and a few monasteries, but perhaps the 'home-made' industry will flourish once again in this age of do-it-yourself.

Drinking Habits

Liqueur-drinking habits have changed relatively little since the 16th century. Brandy, gin and liqueurs were drunk before a meal to whet the appetite, as a digestive after a meal, as a night-cap, or as a treat for one's guests. In his 1683 booklet entitled *The ordinary man's fare; how to live a long and healthy life without sickness*', the physician S. Blankaart, M.D. wrote: 'Brandy, spiced or unspiced, also anise water, lavas, orange water, lemon water, gold water, Dutch gin and the like are all good when taken in moderation either during a meal, after a meal, before or after the drinking of tea.'

Drinking before tea strikes us as a little odd, but even more unusual was the habit of certain groups of people of drinking brandy, usually spiced, before breakfast. This tonic was said to strengthen the stomach, revive the spirit and brighten the day. The habit was ousted by the arrival of tea and coffee, but could still be found in the 19th century, as the following extract from Osgood Mackenzie's 'A Hundred Years in the Highlands' illustrates: 'On the buffet ready for breakfast there was always a bottle of whisky, smuggled of course, full of chamomile flowers, bitter orange peel and juniper berries—bitters we called them— and he (Sir Hector Mackenzie) always had a wee glass before breakfast to strengthen the stomach'.

Even these days apparently, some old East-European families are still sometimes woken up with a glass of Slivovitz.

In the old days when long journeys were made by barge or stagecoach, people liked to take a drink with them. This is evident from the liqueur boxes, made of beautiful wood, and containing about six crystal flasks with various glasses. People used to keep warm and pass the time pleasantly in this way.

English huntsmen, too, would rally themselves with liqueurs. In the time of Queen Victoria their hunting flasks would be filled with cherry brandy!

For centuries a glass of liqueur has been a comfort during hard times. The 18th century Lady Mary Wortley Montagu wrote: 'I am convinced that it is extremely silly to give in to adversity. One should take heart and live on

liqueur if nothing *else* is available:'
and Wilhelm Busch said in *Die Fromme
Helena*:

It has been a custom since days of yore,
He who has worries, also has liqueur.

The finest example of this dates from our
own time. From research into superstition and
magic in the town of Ghent it appears that, in
1960, in the weeks before the world was said
to be ending, liqueur sales increased
enormously!

The labelling of liqueur as a 'woman's drink'
dates from the 17th century when it was
called *the soft, sweet and nice tipple*. This
remained true until well into the 20th century
and even as late as the 1950s women were
still frowned upon if they had cognac or gin
instead of a sweet drink.

Country dwellers continue to drink their
own 'home-brewed' liqueurs. Liqueur is not
an every day drink, but it is nevertheless fairly
popular at christenings, weddings, funerals,
house-warmings, birthdays, celebrations and
parties, and all other such social occasions.

Happily liqueurs have lost their feminine
associations in recent years as men have
rediscovered their fragrance. In 1950
Curnovsky, a French gourmet, described in *La
table et l'amour* how a man should drink a
liqueur: 'One does not drink a liqueur, one
takes it like one takes a woman. One strokes
her with the eyes, lips and tongue, *on la
respire, on l'aspire, on s'en pénètre, on en
soupire*.' (Consult a dictionary for the
translation).

Distillation and Maturation

The high percentage of alcohol in a drink is usually obtained by distillation of a natural fermentation product. Simple fermentation can give an alcohol level of up to 20% in exceptional cases, but usually between 3 and 8%. An alcohol-containing liquid is formed at room temperature because microscopic organisms, yeast cells, spontaneously convert the sugar content of a liquid—fruit juice, for instance—into alcohol. The raw materials for the preparation of alcohol can be divided into two groups: sugar-rich substances such as fruit, sugar-cane, agave, honey and milk; and starchy substances such as grain, maize, rice and potatoes. The starch from the latter group must first be converted into sugar before fermentation can take place. The fermented liquid, which is largely a solution of alcohol in water, serves as the starting material for distillation.

Distilling (from the Latin *distillare* to drip down) is the conversion of liquid into vapour by heating and the liquefaction of this vapour by cooling. By this means, alcohol, which has a lower boiling point than water and con-sequently vapourises more quickly, can be separated from water.

The alcohol-containing mixture is heated in a distillation kettle, and the alcohol vapour is led via the still-head (which closes off the top of the kettle and serves to condense the least volatile component so that it runs back into the kettle) through an outlet tube to the cooling mechanism. This cooling mechanism usually consists of a hollow coil immersed in a water-filled bath, and the liquid is collected at the end of this.

At first this process had to be repeated many times in order to work up a high alcohol level but nowadays there is equipment which can reach a level of 96% in one operation. In the 16th century the alcohol content in a liquid was tested by mixing it with gunpowder and setting the mixture alight. If it burned with an intense flame the drink was too strong. If it remained a sodden, sizzling mass it was too weak. But if it burned with a gentle, even, bluish flame—voilá, a proven spirit. Hence the English expression for alcoholic strength: so many degrees 'proof', which is not the same as a percentage. In the English Sykes system, 175° proof is equal to 100% alcohol (= 100° Gay Lussac) and equal to 200° proof US.

This alcohol percentage is very important to the distiller, because the higher it is, the fewer characteristics remain of the original drink. Among these characteristic substances are fusel oils, esters and aldehydes which, in too large a quantity, give the distillate an unpleasant taste and smell but which should not be entirely absent, or just plain alcohol would result.

The characteristic taste and aroma of a drink are not only determined by the basic ingredients but also develop during the distillation process and maturation in the wood. Through maturation the taste mellows and the aroma is enhanced, while the alcohol absorbs some tannic acid from the wood and the drink acquires a golden tint. Maturation is important mainly for cognac, armagnac, whisky, rum and some types of Dutch gin. Drinks like vodka and gin are distilled to such a high alcohol level that maturation would be of no use. Drinks distilled from fruit are never matured in wood as this would affect the fruit's flavour. The maturation process takes place only in the wood; once a spirituous drink has been bottled it does not mature any more, in contrast to wine. After maturation the drink is blended with older distillates to standardise the quality and aroma. This may be followed by another maturation period after which the drink is bottled.

Conversion of Percentage Alcohol to Degrees Proof (Proof Spirit)

Percentage Alcohol	Proof Spirit (British)	Proof Spirit (U.S.A)
5.0	8.75	10.0
5.7	10.0	11.4
8.6	15.0	17.2
10.0	17.5	20.0
11.4	20.0	22.8
14.3	25.0	28.6
15.0	26.3	30.0
17.2	30.0	34.2
20.0	35.0	40.0
22.8	40.0	45.6
25.0	43.7	50.0
25.7	45.0	51.4
28.5	50.0	57.0
30.0	52.5	60.0
31.4	55.0	62.8
34.2	60.0	68.2
35.0	61.3	70.0
37.0	65.0	74.1
40.0	70.0	80.0

If I had a thousand sons, the first human
principle I would teach them should be, to
foreswear their potations, and to addict
themselves to sack.
William Shakespeare   Henry IV Part 2

Aromatic Ingredients

Processing

The character of a liqueur is not generally determined by the alcohol on which it is based, but by the aromatic ingredients which are dissolved in it. These substances can impart their fragrance and taste to the drink in different ways:

Distilling—first of all the aromatic ingredients such as spices, rinds, seeds and roots are steeped with the fermentation product for a few days, using gentle heat. Then follows the distillation process proper, as described in the previous chapter. For Dutch gins (genevers) and for brandies another method is often used to capture the fragrance and taste of the herbs. These are hung in a basket in the still-head and impart their flavour to the alcohol vapour as it is drawn through them. This results in a much less strong aroma than by the first method.

Digesting—the ingredients are steeped in alcohol at about 70°C so that a complete solution of all the soluble substances is obtained. This is done in a closed kettle under fixed pressure. Chiefly applied in the preparation of bitters.

Percolating—To capture the taste and aroma of beans such as coffee and cocoa, the alcoholic liquid is allowed to trickle slowly through a thick layer of ground beans (with or without heating) just as you make your own coffee.

Macerating—the aromatic substances are allowed to soak in the alcohol for some time, so that the liquid becomes saturated with the smell and taste of the plant or plants. In this way not only the volatile components remain in the alcohol but also other compounds such as resins, fats, bitter substances, acids and proteins. There are in fact plants that do not part with their aromatic components by distillation but do so by this method. The result is an infusion or tincture.

Herbs used in Liqueur Making

Aloe (Aloe vera)
The sap from the leaves is used, which has a

bitter flavour and strange smell. The ancient
Greeks used it as a laxative and (according to
Hippocrates) to ward off the plague.
Angelica (Angelica archangelica)
The root is used and sometimes the seeds
which taste bitter and musky. In folklore it was
associated with heaven (hence the name) and
according to tradition its qualities were
revealed by an angel in a dream during a
plague epidemic. A small piece of the root
was kept in the mouth to drive away the
plague-ridden air.
Anise (Pimpinella anisum)
The seeds are used (aniseed), which are sharp
and taste of liquorice. It is one of the oldest
herbs and is mentioned in the Bible. The
Romans included aniseed in cakes that they
ate to prevent indigestion after a banquet.
They did not have liqueurs then for this
purpose. King Edward IV had his linens
perfumed with it: *Lytil bagges of fustian
stuffed with ireos and anneys* (little bombasine
bags filled with iris and anise).
Arnica (Arnica montana)
The flowers are used, which taste sweet-sour,
or the root which is pungent and bitter and
reminiscent of violets.
Avens (Geum urbanum) Herb Bennet
The seeds and the root are used. It is very
similar to cloves but less strong. An ingredient
of Alpine herb liqueur.
Bay (Laurus nobilis)
The leaves and the berries are used. The
Bedouins of the desert put them in their
coffee. Bay is the symbol of success and glory,

but also a good protector against thunder and
lightning. In the Middle Ages people thought
that the berries had an abortive action. The
shrub came into existence when Apollo
pursued the nymph Daphne, who constantly
denied him. The Gods were merciful to her
and turned her into a bay tree!
Bergamot (Citrus bergamia)
Bergamot apple can be obtained as oil or
tincture. Its perfume resembles that of the
bergamot plant (*Monarda didyma*) which bees
find very attractive. One of the most fragrant
herbs.
Caraway (Carum carvi) Kümmel
The strong-tasting seeds are used. It is the
oldest indigenous European herb; seeds of it
have been found in the remains of pile-
dwellings in Switzerland. Its use was widespread in love-potions, and a Greek physician
from the 1st century prescribed it to girls with
pale faces. It is the most important ingredient
in Kümmel (a Dutch liqueur).
Cardamom (Elettaria cardamomum)
The seeds are used; they taste very aromatic
and fiery but at the same time refreshing. By
as early as the 4th century BC the Greeks
were importing it from Indonesia. In Arabic
countries it is often put in coffee and the
Arabs have a profound belief in the power of
cardamom as a love-potion.
Celery (Apium graveolens)
Usually the root is used, but the seeds are
used too. Often found in love-potions.
Chamomile (Matricaria chamomilla)
The flowers are used. They are blended into

bénédictine and chartreuse.

Chicory (Cichorium intybus)
The root is used, which is spicy and has a bitter flavour. It is often used as a coffee substitute.

Cinnamon (Cinnamomum zeylanicum)
The bark and the twigs are used. There are various kinds of cinnamon, but in Europe the Ceylonese kind predominates. Cinnamon ranks among the very ancient spices and is mentioned in Exodus 30:23-25, where God ordered Moses to rub a mixture of cinnamon, sweet flag, cinnamon bark, myrrh and oil into the tabernacle. For a long time cinnamon was used as an aphrodisiac.

Cloves (Eugenia caryophyllata)
The scarcely-developed flower buds are used. These are antiseptic and, amongst other things, relieve toothache.

Cochineal (Coctus cacti)
This is a scarlet scale insect. The dried insects are used for colouring.

Coriander (Coriandrum sativum)
The seeds are used. These have been found in Egyptian graves and are mentioned in Exodux 16:31. *The Arabian Nights* mention coriander as a passion stimulant, and in the Middle Ages too, people were persuaded of this quality. An ingredient of Eau des Carmes.

Cummin (Cuminum cyminum)
The seeds are used; the taste resembles caraway and cummin is very often confused with it. Cummin has been known since time immemorial. Isaiah 28:27 describes how cummin was threshed with a stick. This still happens today in the same way on primitive farms in the Middle-East.

Dill (Anethum graveolens)
The seeds are used, which have a spicy aromatic flavour, somewhat like caraway seeds. In Saxon times dill seeds were given to babies, with water, to settle them. It was a weapon against witchcraft and an important ingredient of love potions.

Elecampane (Inula helenium)
The root is used, it has a bitter taste and smells somewhat like violets when dried. it was a famous medicinal plant in former times. The Greeks called it *helenion* because it was supposed to have sprung from Helen's tears.

Fennel (Anethum foeniculum)
The seeds are used, which have a slightly aniseed-like aroma. Fennel is very old—the Chinese, Indians and Egyptians were familiar with it. In the Middle Ages it was thought to be effective against evil spirits.

Galangal (Alpinia galanga and Alpinia officinarum)
The root is used; it has a sharp and bitter flavour. It is often sold under the Malayan name of *laos*.

Gentian (Gentiana lutea)
The root is used and has a bitter flavour.

Ginger (Zingiber officinale)
The root is used, which tastes sharp. It was one of the first eastern spices to be exported to Europe. In the Koran a ginger drink is mentioned which was drunk in Paradise (Koran 76:17). In the time of Queen Elizabeth I gingerbread was very popular and Shake-

speare mentions it in his works. In England a popular drink is made by putting ginger in beer: *ginger ale*.

Iris (Iris florentina)
Florentine white flag, violet root. The root is used, which smells strongly of violets. The *poudre de riz* (d'Iris), a face powder was made from this in former times.

Juniper berry (Juniperus communis)
The berries are used. Genever (Dutch gin) owes its name to it, as does English gin. They are appetisers.

Lemon balm (Melissa officinalis)
The herb is used, which has a lemon-like, somewhat bitter flavour. Pliny claimed this plant was a remedy against hysteria.

Liquorice (Glycyrrhiza glabra)
The roots and shoots are used. An old remedy for thirst. Napolen chewed lots of it, which made his teeth go black.

Litmus
A red-blue dye obtained from lichens.

Lovage (Levisticum officinale)
The root is used, which has a meaty taste. Mainly in bitters.

Mace, nutmeg blossom, macis or nutmeg bark
This is the pulpy skin of the nutmeg fruit, the kernel being the actual nutmeg. Mace has the same flavour as nutmeg, but is a little sharper and more aromatic. The Gourmet Werumeus Buning wrote that 'stewing-steak without mace is like a ship without a rudder'.

Marjoram (Origanum majorana) Sweet marjorum
The herb is used. It symbolises happiness, and the Ancient Greeks considered that marjoram growing on a grave was a sign of bliss for the dead. It used to be spread over the floor as an air freshener and it was also regarded as a protection against witches.

Mint (Mentha crispa) Curled mint
The leaves are used, which clearly have a different taste to peppermint, being more caraway-like. Amongst other things an ingredient of bénédictine.

Myrrh (Commiphora molmol)
This is the gum resin of the myrrh balsam tree. Obtainable as a tincture (solution in alcohol).

Nutmeg
This is the seed kernel of the fruit from the nutmeg tree (*Myristica fragans*). For a long time hippies used nutmeg because, when taken in very large quantities, it had a strong sedative and intoxicating effect. However, the hangover was so bad that they stopped taking it. Nutmeg is mentioned repeatedly as a medicine in India's holy Vedic writings.

Pepper (Pipe nigrum)
The seeds are used; unripe ones for black pepper, ripe ones for white pepper. It used to be a very rare and expensive herb; as valuable as gold and silver. In the Middle Ages people used it to pay for things, including dowries, rent, tax and leases. Pepper is one of the oldest herbs and was mentioned in the Sanskrit writings. It was regarded as a stimulant.

Peppermint (Mentha piperata)
The leaves and the flowering herb are used.

Its cool taste lends itself extremely well to liqueurs; in bénédictine, chartreuse and bitters.
Pimento (Pimento officinalis) Jamaica pepper or allspice
The unripe fruits are used. The taste is like a mixture of cinnamon, cloves and nutmeg, hence the English call it *allspice*. Pimento was used on board ships to preserve meat, and this is still done in Scandanavia, with fish. Important in bénédictine and chartreuse.
Quinquina (Cinchona)
The bark is used, which tastes bitter. It has febrifugal qualities and because it was so expensive was often faked with red-coloured oak bark.
Rosemary (Rosmarinus officinalis)
The leaves and flowers are used. Symbol of friendship and remembrance. There are many legends about rosemary. In the Middle Ages it protected people against the evil eye, witches and the Devil. The first ethereal oils were distilled from rosemary by Raymond Lulle in 1330. In ancient times rosemary was also burned as incense. It is an important ingredient in eau de cologne and Eau de la reine d'Hongrie.
Sage (Salvia officinalis)
The leaves are used. It used to be thought that sage increased fertility and lengthened lives. An ingredient of chartreuse.
Saffron (Crocus sativus)
The stigmas are used. The ancient Egyptians were already acquainted with saffron, and in the 1st century Pliny warned against faking with marigold leaves.

It has always been rare and expensive and is still the most expensive herb. Saffron has been used since primeval times to induce labour or abortion in women. It also seemed to have a cheering effect on people.
Sandalwood (Lignum santali rubrum)
The red heart-wood is used. White sandalwood also exists. Sandalwood was mentioned in the Sanskrit writings and was used, amongst other things, as colouring.
Star anise (Illicium anisatum)
The ripe fruits are used, the seed-bearing structures of which are star-shaped. The taste is the same as *Pimpinella anise*, but a little sharper. Used in liqueur along with aniseed.
Sugar root see Chicory
Sweet flag (Acorus calamus)
The root is used, which has a sharp flavour. In Arabia and Iran it is used to make love potions.
Thyme (Thymus vulgaris)
The sprigs with leaves are used. A symbol of courage and bravery. In England thyme is said to be a favourite with fairies. Hence the old recipe made with this herb, which enables one to see these creatures. Thyme is good for nightmares and hangovers. In herbal and bitter liqueurs.
Turmeric (Curcuma longa) Curcuma or Indonesian saffron
The root is used, which has a pungent peppery flavour reminiscent of mustard and ginger. It gives a yellow-orange colour and in Indonesia, amongst other things, was used at wedding rituals, to paint the bride's and

groom's arms yellow. In many Far East
countries it was used as make-up to give a
golden complexion.

Vanilla (Vanilla planifolia)
The long pods are used. They are coated with
cocoa butter and dried.

*Wormwood (Artemisia absinthium) green
ginger*
The herb is used, which has a very bitter taste.
The sale of this plant is prohibited in many
countries because it poisons the central
nervous system and continuous use causes a
degeneration process which cannot be reversed.

Herbs that appear in old recipes but are now
rarely used include: Chervil, woodruff, spear-
mint, basil, savoury, tarragon, centaury, hyssop
and blessed thistle.

Advice

All the measurements given in the recipes for making your own liqueurs are merely guide-lines; the extent to which you follow them will depend on your individual taste and the availability of raw materials.

As the distilling of alcohol is prohibited almost everywhere, I have not given any recipes or instructions for this. Should you wish to evade the law, I refer you to the professional literature.

The alcohol

The alcoholic base that you choose for your liqueur depends on your preferences and the aromatic ingredients that you are going to use. Each class of distilled drinks has its own taste and smell, but this can vary from product to product. Take, for instance, all the different kinds of gin, whisky and brandy. Using these characteristic tastes, you can compose some very subtle combinations but you have to know exactly what you are doing. One way of avoiding mistakes is to fill a number of small bottles with the same aromatic ingredients and add different drinks to them. Or the same

drink and different aromatic ingredients, or different proportions. Carefully note on each bottle what you did, to enable you to make the nicest one again sometime.

A simpler but less reliable method is by smell. The role that your nose plays in liqueur preparation is at least as important as your sense of taste, for it is a pleasure, is it not? to sniff a liqueur's bouquet before letting the liquid glide over your tongue!

The safest method is to use rectified spirit (rectified ethyl alcohol). This is sold in its undiluted form—between 90 and 96%—or diluted with various amounts of distilled water by chemists with licences to sell spirits (but not all have this licence). Make sure you ask for rectified spirit at the chemist, because other sorts of alcohol are very dangerous in spite of their seemingly agreeable qualities.

This method of liqueur-making is however no cheaper than buying ordinary drinks from a wine shop as VAT, excise duties and the chemist's profits are all very high!

An excellent base-drink with little flavour is vodka. I prefer this to brandy which is always slightly acid, especially for fruits in alcohol. But it is purely a matter of taste.

Next to vodka, eau de vie is a good base for liqueurs. It is less acid than brandy and nowadays costs about the same. Do use the white eau de vie though, it is purer than the coloured variety. Armagnac and cognac combined with fruits are a real delicacy but a very expensive one. The price of a glass of cognac or armagnac is nearly twice that of a glass of eau de vie, brandy or vodka. However, if you can befriend a chemist or pharmacist, or can come by cheap alcohol in some other way, then liqueur-making can even become profitable. (Duty-free shops and holidays abroad also defray expenses.)

Below is a list of the most important distilled drinks.

Drinks distilled from grapes

Armagnac comes from the land of the Three Musketeers, the French department of Gers. The young wine, prepared from Ugni Blanc, Folle Blanche or Colombar grapes, is single distilled and then has to mature in black oak barrels from the Gascogne.

There are three regions: Bas-Armagnac, Ténarèze and Hau-Armagnac. A bottle labelled 'Armagnac' only is usually a mixture from all three regions.

Hors d'âge means that the drink is at least 25 years old and VSOP (Very Superior Old Pale) means at least four years old.

Cognac comes only from a certain part of the French Charente. Charente inférieur is prepared from the same grapes as armagnac. The difference is that the wine is distilled twice and has to mature in oak barrels from Limoges or Tronçais. There are seven *cru* (vineyards) which encircle the city of Cognac. Starting from the middle: Grande Champagne, Petite Champagne, Borderies, Fins Bois, Bons Bois, Bois Ordinaires and Bois à Terroir. For VSOP and Hors d'âge: see Armagnac. In the old days, stars on a bottle meant that the shipper who transported cognac guaranteed its quality.

Eau de vie (de vin) is sometimes called brandy and is distilled from a brandy-type wine that does not come from the armagnac or cognac areas.

Marc is distilled from grape pips and skins which are mixed with water and fermented after the grapes have been pressed. The Marc de Bourgogne and the Marc de Champagne are the most famous.

Drinks distilled from fruit

Calvados brandy distilled from Normandy apples.

Fraise (Eau de vie de fraises) brandy distilled from strawberries.

Framboise (Eau de vie de framboises) brandy distilled from raspberries.

Kirsch brandy distilled from cherries and cherry pips.

Mirabelle (Eau de vie de mirabelles) brandy distilled from plums.

Poire Williams (Williamsbirne) brandy distilled from Williams pears, the most famous of the pear brandies.

Prune (Eau de vie de prunes) brandy distilled from plums.

Slivovitz brandy distilled from Balkan plums. One of the few fruit distillates that do mature in the wood.

Drinks distilled from grain, sugar-beet or potatoes

Aquavit (Akvavit) brandy distilled from grain or potatoes and then distilled with caraway seeds.

Brandy used to be distilled from grain, but now the alcohol is recovered from slightly acid ingredients. A typical example is filtering through beech or alder charcoal, which was formerly used to extract certain impurities but now gives its special flavour.

Eau de vie (de grains) French brandy distilled from grain.

Genever (Dutch gin) is prepared by recovering grain or molasses alcohol from a mixture containing juniper berries and other herbs. Old genever means genever made according to the old method, with more malt-wine than the young genever and sometimes 'lagered' (matured). Young genever is not sweetened or coloured and is hardly matured.

Dubbelgebeide genever which has been twice distilled over juniper berries or double the quantity has been used.

Whisky every whisky is distilled from fermented grain, by and large from malted barley, maize and rye. Scotch whisky is distilled from malted barley with or without other grains. Irish whiskey comes from the same grains as Scottish whisky, but a certain percentage of oats is often included. Bourbon whisky or whiskey (from the United States) is distilled from fermented grains with no less than 51% maize. Rye whisky should be distilled from at least 51% rye.

Vodka can be distilled from any raw material, as it is distilled to such a high percentage of alcohol that hardly any of the other ingredients' characteristics remain. Then the alcohol is filtered through charcoal, to make it even purer. Certain vodkas from Russia and Poland are flavoured with herbs and 'lagered'. Vodka, like aquavit, should be drunk in one swig and ice cold.

Drinks distilled from sugar canes etc.

Arak comes from the Far East and is usually distilled from various ingredients such as palm juice, dates and coconut milk.

Rum was originally distilled from sugar-cane but is nowadays mostly from molasses, a by-product of sugar production.

Tequila from Mexico is prepared from pulque, the fermented juice of a desert cactus, the blue agave.

Sweetening

For sweetening, ordinary granulated sugar is eminently suitable. Sugar-candy is recommended in many old recipes, because it was purer than ordinary sugar and had a more pleasant flavour. Today this difference is no longer of importance. However, sugar-candy gives a slightly more syrupy result than ordinary sugar. Loaf sugar (sugar which is poured into a cone-shaped mould) was recommended for the same reason.

Honey is delicious in liqueur and gives a completely different taste. The only drawback is that it is so expensive. In many recipes which I have read, sugar is boiled into syrup with water and cooled before being added to the liqueur. The advantage of this method is that the sugar is well-dissolved before it is put into the drink, but a disadvantage (which for me is more important) is that the liqueur becomes too diluted by the addition of the water with which the syrup has been prepared. I do not recommend this procedure except when using undiluted rectified spirit. Generally speaking, the sugar is not added until after filtering, and you should then shake the bottle a few times to let it dissolve. It is better not to add sugar to the alcohol at the same time as the aromatic ingredients, because the latter yield their aroma better to an unsweetened alcohol. Otherwise, they become 'candied'. (Of course, this does not apply to fruits in alcohol, which, on the contrary, are enhanced by this method.) The famous twigs with sugar crystals which can be seen in certain German and Italian liqueurs, are very easy to make yourself.

Make a syrup by heating 0.5 kilo (1 lb) of sugar with ¼ litre (½ pint) of water, stirring well; bring to the boil and leave to simmer for a few minutes, but make sure it does not colour, it should definitely stay clear. Let the syrup cool and mix it with the same quantity of alcoholic drink (e.g. an already prepared kümmel, mint or aniseed liqueur) of about 80%. Put a few well-shaped twigs in a clear bottle and pour in the liqueur. The sugar crystals will automatically attach themselves to the twigs. The effect is extremely attractive, but the liqueur is extremely sweet! To avoid crystallisation of sugar in your alcohol, add a drop of lemon or tartaric acid to the syrup and let it simmer for about 10 minutes.

Macerating or extracting

The amount of time the fruits, herbs or flowers have to be left to soak in the alcohol is indicated in each recipe. It is only an approximation, depending on the weather conditions, the number of aromatic ingredients and the place where the bottle or jar is stored. Opinions differ about the temperature at which maceration should take place. Some say it should be in a cool dark place, but others say it should be in a warm light spot.

Herbs will macerate well in a moderately warm temperature, but some soft fruits are better left a bit longer in a cool place. I myself put the extracts on a high shelf in my kitchen so that I have them handy and can shake them from time to time. This shaking is very important in order to get a good extract.

Filtering

A liqueur should be crystal-clear and therefore filtering is important. A strong paper filter will do the job very nicely. However, a nylon filter is better, as this does not tear if you, like me, feel inclined to squeeze the last drops out of it. For liqueurs that are prepared with fruit juice a nylon filter is imperative. Should the liqueur not be completely clear after maturation, then filter it once again. If there is some sediment on the bottom then you had best decant the liqueur. This means carefully pouring the drink into another bottle, so that the dregs are left in the bottom.

Glassware

The preserving jars or bottles should be spotlessly clean. There should be no trace of soap or of the previous contents. To ensure this, soak the glassware in soda water for half an hour and clean it thoroughly with a brush. Then rinse it in hot water and leave to drip dry, upside-down.

Corks can be cleaned by soaking them in boiling water for 10 to 15 minutes. Rinse them and let them dry completely before you use them. When using preserving jars you should make sure they are air-tight, because alcohol evaporates quickly.

Colouring

A liqueur is not improved by attractive colouring, but it does look more tempting. Many liqueurs already have a good colour from certain herbs and fruits, but you can give nature a helping hand by adding a harmless, edible dye. It should have no smell and no taste. These colourings can be bought from a chemist or supermarket. A brown colour with a slight caramel taste can be obtained by substituting part of the sugar by brown sugar. Curaçao is tinged by lightly grilling the orange peel before adding it to the alcohol.

Maturing and storing

After the liqueur has been bottled it should be left to mature for some time, to give the aroma time to develop to the full. Here 'the longer the better' applies. After a year a liqueur is excellent, but after a few years it has an even rounder and more fragrant flavour.

Fruits in alcohol are the only exception because some fruits, like strawberries, become far too soft and are no longer good to eat. For the impatient among you there is a trick. If you dissolve ⅓ gram of tartaric acid in a little water and add this to 1 litre (2 pints) of liqueur, it will taste as good in a few days as after 6 months. Keep the bottles in a cool dark place. Once a bottle of liqueur has been opened it will keep for a long time, if you put the top back on properly.

Ratafias and Fruits in Alcohol

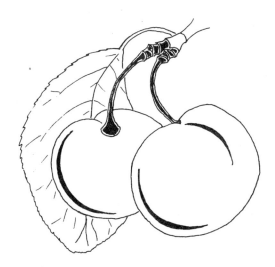

It is most important to use fresh, ripe fruits, but do make sure they're not too ripe. They should be sound, without bruises and free from maggots. Unsprayed fruit are preferable, but usually difficult to come by. The washed fruit must be dried so that the liqueur does not become too watery. If the skins are to be used in a recipe, the fruit must be well-scrubbed with water and wiped dry before you skin them. The rinds from citrus fruits must not have any pith attached, so peel them thinly and carefuly.

Fruit juice can be prepared in a number of ways:

1   Strain the fruits, cut into small pieces if necessary, through a sieve, or squeeze them through a cloth.

2.   Add a little water or wine to the washed fruit and bring to the boil. Leave to simmer until juice starts exuding from the fruit, remove from the heat and strain through a sieve or squeeze through a cloth.

3.   If you own a centrifuge or a special kettle, then follow the maker's instructions.

With ratafias, because of the addition of fruit juice, the alcohol level of the liqueur ends up lower than the 35–45% you started off with. Usually it falls to around 25%. Those who like it stronger can correct this by adding ¼ litre (½ pint) or more of 90–96% alcohol to each litre. You then get a liqueur of about 33%.

Whole fruits also release juice and so the same applies as for ratafias.

I have included many varieties of recipe in this book, but there are countless other possibilities. You can put different herbs with the fruits, combine fruits, take other distilled drinks and change — or even completely omit — the amount of sugar.

Almond *(Amygdalus communis)*

The fruit of the shrub, originally from Syria. It can be found as an ornamental shrub but this variety does not often bear fruit because it blooms early and is caught by frost. There are bitter and sweet almonds. You must be careful when eating bitter almonds because they contain cyanide (prussic acid), a very poisonous substance. Instead of almonds or bitter almonds you can safely use a good almond essence.

Almond liqueur I

250 gm (½ lb) sweet almonds
1 tsp cinnamon
1 tsp cloves
5 tsp bitter orange rind
350 gm (¾ lb) sugar
1 litre (2 pints) brandy or eau de vie

Chop the almonds or crush them finely. Add the eau de vie or brandy and let the mixture stand for a month. Shake from time to time. Then filter and add the sugar. Shake once a day until the sugar has dissolved and leave to mature for at least another 2 months.

Almond liqueur II

200 gm (7 oz) sweet almonds
50 gm (1¾ oz) bitter almonds
10 gm orange blossom water
1 tsp mace
1 tsp cinnamon
some lemon rind
400 gm (13¾ oz) sugar
1 litre (2 pints) eau de vie

For the preparation see *Almond liqueur I.*

Scottish almond liqueur (Scots noyau)

200 gm (7 oz) sweet almonds
35 gm (1¼ oz) bitter almonds
¼ litre (½ pint) syrup
1 bottle Scotch whisky

Blanch the almonds (immerse them briefly in boiling water and peel off the skins) and grind them with a little whisky in a mortar until fine. This is to prevent the oil from separating. Let the ingredients stand together for 14 days. Shake from time to time. Then filter and bottle.

English noyau

almond essence to taste
350 gm (¾ lb) sugar
1 litre (2 pints) London gin

For the preparation see *Scots noyau.*

Almond shrub (Crème d'amandes) from the 18th century cookery book by John Luff

Take 1 litre (2 pints) of rum or brandy, ¼ litre (½ pint) of orange juice and 125 gm (4½ oz) of sugar. Then take 10 gm (⅓ oz) of bitter almonds, blanch them and crush them. Mix the almond paste with ¼ cupful of milk, add the other ingredients and stir well. Leave for about an hour to curdle, strain a few times through a flannel cloth until clear and bottle for use.

Apricot *(Prunus armeniaca)*

An orange, stoned fruit.
Picking season June–July
Habitat In Northern Europe, Canada and the Northern States of USA only in orangeries and glasshouses.

Apricots in brandy

1 kilo (2 lb) fresh apricots
a little white wine
0.5 kilo (1 lb) sugar
1 litre (2 pints) brandy

Pierce the apricots a few times with a fork or darning needle. Bring a saucepan of water to the boil, add the apricots and leave to simmer for about 2 minutes. Strain off the boiling water and run cold water over the fruit. Leave in this water for 10 minutes, then drain. Peel the apricots, halve them and remove the stones. Crack the stones and take out the kernels. Make a syrup with the sugar and some white wine and throw in the apricots and the kernels. Bring once more to the boil, sieve out the apricots with a straining spoon and put them aside in a preserving jar. The syrup should be left to simmer so that it thickens. Cool and pour over the apricots. Add the brandy and close the jar tightly. Wait for 2–3 months before you taste it.

Variation use ¾ litre (1½ pints) brandy and ¼ litre (½ pint) apricot brandy.

Apricots in eau de vie

0.75 kilo (1½ lb) fresh apricots
250 gm (½ lb) sugar
¾ litre (1½ pints) eau de vie
a few almonds and/or a few grains of paradise seed (optional)

Peel the apricots and halve them. Take out the stones, crack them and remove the kernels. Cut them into small pieces, along with the almonds, add the paradise seed and tie them together in a piece of muslin. Place the halved apricots and the muslin bag in a preserving jar, sprinkle the sugar on top and cover with eau de vie. Let the pot stand, securely closed, for 3 to 4 months, but shake it now and again.

Boerenmeisjes

300 gm (10 oz) dried apricots
sugar to taste
rind of a lemon
cinnamon stick
¼ litre (½ pint) water
1 litre (2 pints) preserving brandy

Let the apricots soak in the water for 24 hours. Then add the sugar and the herbs, bring to the boil and leave to simmer for about 10 minutes. Cool. Put the apricots with the syrup into a preserving jar and add the brandy. Leave the jar for 3 months.

Apricot ratafia

½ litre (1 pint) mashed apricots
300 gm (9¾ oz) sugar
rind of an orange
rind of half a lemon
eau de vie

After the stones have been removed from the apricots squeeze them in a linen cloth with the aid of a hand press. Add the juice together with the sugar and the rind to the eau de vie and leave in a warm place for 6 weeks. Then filter and store making sure that the container is securely closed.

Apricots in vodka

300 gm (9¾ oz) dried apricots
¼ litre (½ pint) white wine
rind of half a lemon
a few bitter or sweet almonds, chopped
a piece of cinnamon stick
300 gm (9¾ oz) sugar
1 litre (2 pints) vodka

For preparation see *Boerenmeisjes*.

Bilberry *(Vaccinium myrtillus)*

A small, red, somewhat bitter berry. Also called whortleberry and blueberry.
Picking season September–October
Habitat On sandy soil, in woods and on heaths.

Bilberry liqueur

For the preparation and measurements see cranberry liqueur.

Blackberry *(Rubus fruticosus)*

A red or black fruit, also called bramble.
Picking season August to October
Habitat In hedges, alongside roads, on the edges of woods and dunes and in the undergrowth. Also cultivated.

Blackberries in brandy

0.5 kilo (1 lb) blackberries
200 gm (7 oz) sugar
a piece of lemon rind
¾ litre (1½ pints) preserving brandy

Clean the berries thoroughly and put them in a preserving jar. Sprinkle the sugar on top and add the lemon rind and some allspice (optional). Pour the brandy over the berries and close the jar tightly. Shake carefully from time to time. Do not open for at least 2 weeks, but better still, leave to mature for another month.

Blackberry whisky

0.5 kilo (1 lb) blackberries
100 gm (3½ oz) sugar
a few cloves
a piece of cinnamon stick
1 bottle whisky

Put the washed berries in a preserving jar or pot. Mash them a little with a fork, sprinkle sugar over the top and add the herbs. Pour over the whisky to cover and close the jar. Shake occasionally. After 2 months filter the blackberry whisky and taste to check if it is sweet enough. Bottle.

Blackcurrant *(Ribes nigrum)*

A small, black sweet-sour berry. Also called cassis.
Picking season July
Habitat cultivated, usually in kitchen gardens. According to the French, liqueur prepared from these berries is *par excellence* and is also the healthiest. Cassis liqueur is at its best after 3 to 4 years.

Blackcurrants in brandy

0.75 kilo (1½ lb) blackcurrants
half a lemon
300 gm (10 oz) brown sugar or sugar candy
brandy

Put the washed and stripped berries in a

preserving bottle together with the rind and juice of half a lemon. Add the sugar or sugar candy and cover the mixture liberally with brandy. Seal and do not open for at least 3 months.

Variation leave out the sugar and use Dutch gin instead of brandy.

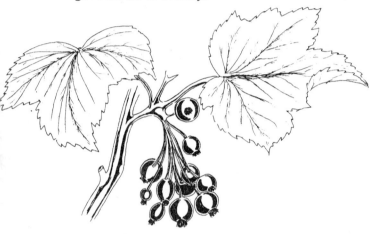

Blackcurrant ratafia

0.4 litre (1 pint) blackcurrant juice
0.1 litre (¼ pint) bird cherry juice
1½ tsp cinnamon
2 tsp paradise seed
1 litre (2 pints) 50% rectified spirit
sugar to taste

Let all the ingredients except the sugar soak together for 6 weeks. Filter and add the sugar. Preferably let the ratafia mature for a further 6 months. However, it can be drunk immediately.

Cassis liqueur

Wash and dry 100 gm (3½ oz) of raspberries and 0.6 kilo (1 lb 4 oz) of blackcurrants. Pound them thoroughly, cover with a cloth and leave in a cool place for 24 hours. Then add a handful of blackcurrant leaves and ½ litre (1 pint) of rectified spirit. Cover the bowl with a plate so that it is air-tight and leave for another 24 hours. Strain the mush through a cloth and squeeze out well. Dissolve 0.5 kilo (1 lb) sugar in ¼ litre (½ pint) of water or wine by letting it boil gently for 5 minutes. When cool, pour it over the blackcurrant drink and leave covered for another few hours. Filter and bottle.

Cassis ratafia

300 gm (9¾ oz) crushed blackcurrants
25 gm (1 oz) blackcurrant leaves
1 tsp cinnamon
½ tsp cloves
½ tsp coriander
150 gm (5 oz) sugar
¾ litre (1½ pints) eau de vie

Let the ingredients, except the sugar, stand in a well-sealed bottle for 14 days. Strain through a cloth and squeeze out well. Add sugar and bottle.

Variation use vanilla instead of the coriander and cloves.

Cherry *(Prunus avium)*

Picking season May–June
Habitat cultivated or wild
Cherry liqueur, usually called Cherry Brandy, has been a very popular drink for centuries. The Russian empress Elizabeth Petrovna is said to have been addicted to it and the story goes that her need for this drink was as insatiable as her need for love.

Cherry liqueur

½ litre (1 pint) cherry juice (from sweet black cherries)
350 gm (¾ lb) sugar
1 litre (2 pints) brandy or eau de vie
almond essence or a few almonds
cinnamon
cloves and coriander
or
angelica root and ginger

Put all the ingredients together and let them soak for 4 weeks. Filter and bottle.

Cherry ratafia I

0.8 kilo (1 lb 10 oz) cherries or May cherries
350 gm (¾ lb) sugar
1 litre (2 pints) eau de vie
rind of a lemon (optional)
vanilla
cinnamon

Crush the cherries (pips and all) in a bowl (careful, for they splash a lot). Cover the bowl

with a cloth and put in a warmish place. Leave the cherry pulp to ferment for 3 to 4 days. When it has stopped fermenting, add the eau de vie, sugar and, if you like, the herbs, and transfer to a well-sealed jar. Leave for a month. Then pour through a cloth and squeeze well to remove all the juice. Filter again, this time through a paper filter, and bottle.

Cherry ratafia II

0.8 kilo (1 lb 10 oz) cherries
150 gm (6 oz) raspberries
cinnamon, cloves, mace (or just some allspice)
rind of a lemon
350 gm (¾ lb) sugar
1 litre (2 pints) vodka or rum

Crush the cherries with the pips, likewise the raspberries, and add all the herbs. Cover with the alcohol and leave in a tightly closed jar for a month. Pour through a cloth and squeeze out well. Add sugar and after 14 days filter and bottle.

Variation leave out the raspberries and for a real luxury drink use framboise instead of the vodka or rum: eau de vie is nice, too.

Cherries in whisky

0.5 kilo (1 lb) cherries
a few cloves
50 gm (2 oz) sugar
1 bottle whisky

For preparation see Cherries in eau de vie. The drink is nicest with dark sweet cherries. If you must use a rather sour cherry, then add a little more sugar. However, this drink should not be too sweet.

Cherries in eau de vie (from a French recipe of 1807)

0.5 kilo (1 lb) cherries
a piece of cinnamon stick
24 coriander seeds
2 blades of mace
a small piece of tailed pepper
(or 2 peppercorns)
125–250 gm (3½–8 oz) sugar
1 litre (2 pints) eau de vie

Wash the cherries and cut off half the stalks. Put them in a jar with the spices, tied together in a piece of muslin, on top. Sprinkle sugar on the cherries and fill up with eau de vie. Cover the jar securely and leave to stand for 2 to 3 months. Taste a little to see if it is to your liking and then remove the herbs. If it is too spicy for you add some eau de vie and sugar to taste. Bottle.

Bird cherry (Prunus padus)

Small black wild cherry
Picking season August–September
Habitat in woods, hedges, parks and in plantations

Bird cherry liqueur

0.5 kilo (1 lb) bird cherries
400 gm (14 oz) sugar
1 litre (2 pints) eau de vie
Optional:
cloves
cinnamon
bird-cherry leaves
lemon rind

Mash the cherries and their pips and put them in a preserving bottle. Add the herbs and pour brandy over the mush. Let the drink stand for 6 weeks. Sieve the drink through a cloth and squeeze the juice out thoroughly. Finally add the sugar, and do not filter until it is dissolved. Bottle and preferably leave for half a year.

Maraschino-Zara liqueur

0.5 kilo (1 lb) bird cherries
100 gm (3½ oz) raspberries
25 gm (1 oz) cherry leaves
1 tsp iris powder
a few peach stones
0.5 kilo (1 lb) sugar, white or brown
1 litre (2 pints) vodka

Crush the bird cherries, pips and all, and likewise the raspberries. Crack the peach stones. Put all the ingredients except the sugar in a preserving jar, cover securely and leave to stand for 6 weeks. Sieve through a cloth so that you can squeeze all the alcohol out. Add the sugar and when it has dissolved filter the liqueur. Bottle and leave to mature for a further 3 months.

Variation leave out raspberries and iris powder and add some vanilla, cloves, lemon rind and a few sliced dried figs. Or leave out raspberries and iris powder and add a bay leaf and rosewater.

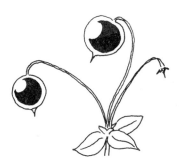

Cranberry (*Oxycoccus palustris*)

A red and rather large berry-like fruit.
Picking season August–October
Habitat quite rare, in fenland and moor-peat marshes.

Cranberry liqueur

Fill a preserving jar ⅔ full with cranberries. Cover with brandy and leave to soak for 3 months, securely closed. Filter the drink and if necessary add sugar to taste.

Variation Add a few herbs and let these soak with the rest. Or use Dutch gin instead of brandy.

Put all the ingredients except the sugar in a preserving jar or large bottle and leave them to soak for 4 weeks. Next, filter the mixture and add the sugar. Leave to mature for at least another 2 months.

You can also bring the currants, sugar and herbs to the boil with a little water, and pour the cooled and strained juice into the eau de vie. The drink becomes drinkable more quickly if prepared by the latter method.

Scottish white currant liqueur Highland cordial

0.5 kilo (1 lb) white currants
peel of a lemon
some ginger essence, root or powder
350 gm (¾ lb) sugar
1 bottle whisky

Wash and strip the currants. Put them in a preserving jar and crush them a little with a fork or spoon. Add the lemon rind, the ginger and the whisky and leave to soak for 2 weeks. Shake the jar from time to time. Filter and add the sugar. After 2 months the liqueur is fit for drinking but it can be kept longer.

Currant liqueur English Royal Cookbook (about 1860)

Press the currants through a coarse cloth. Take half a litre (1 pint) of the juice and add a litre (2 pints) of rum and 100 gm (3½ oz) of sugar. You can use more sugar if you like. Mix well and filter. Bottle.

Variation Instead of rum use Dutch gin.

Red or white currant *(Ribes rubrum)*

Both have a sweet-sour flavour
Picking season May–June
Habitat cultivated and in kitchen gardens

Red currant ratafia

½ litre (1 pint) red currant juice
2 tsp cinnamon
1 tsp nutmeg
1 tsp cloves
lemon peel
0.5 kilo (1 lb) sugar
1 litre (2 pints) eau de vie

Dates *(Phoenix dactylifera)*

The sweet fruit of the date palm is dried and preserved, but can occasionally be bought fresh.

Dates in rum

Take dried or preserved dates. Fill ¾ of a jar or bottle and generously pour the rum over. Leave for a few months, filter and add sugar to taste.

The left-over dates are a delicacy in puddings and custards, or with a dollop of slightly-sweetened whipped cream.

Grape *(Vitis vinifera)*

Picking season September
Habitat cultivated in glasshouses and in warm sheltered places.

Grapes in brandy

Use good, sound, ripe white grapes. Do not wash them but carefully wipe them clean with a cloth. Take them off the bunch and put them in a preserving jar: do not fill more than ¾ full. Pour over a liberal amount of brandy and add 4 peppercorns, 2 cloves and half a vanilla stick. Leave for 3 weeks, shaking occasionally. Then add sugar to taste and leave to mature, preferably for another 3 months.

Variation use eau de vie instead of brandy and a small cinnamon stick instead of the vanilla and peppercorns.

Muscatels in Marc

1 kilo (2 lb) muscatels
150-250 gm (5¼-8 oz) sugar
some mace
1 bottle marc

For the preparation see *grapes in brandy.*

Variation use less grapes and add 250 gm (½ lb) of fresh walnuts, stripping off the wood and bitter skins. This is done more easily with so-called green nuts, which can be bought in September/October.

Grapefruit *(Citrus decumana)*

A bitter, sweet-sour fruit.

Grapefruit whisky

2 grapefruits
a few pieces of orange rind
a few sweet almonds
1 bottle whisky

Wash the grapefruits well and dry them. Cut off a number of very thin pieces of rind and put them in a preserving jar. Cut the fruit into segments (preferably also removing the membranes between them) and put them into the jar, with the orange rind and chopped almonds. Pour in the whisky and leave, well-sealed, for 4 weeks. Strain off the drink, filter it and, if necessary, sweeten with sugar.

You can use the remaining grapefruit segments for a fruit salad or in a cocktail with crab and mayonnaise.

Lemon *(Citrus media)*

A South-European citrus fruit that can be bought the whole year round.

Lemon brandy

rind of 3 lemons
some cinnamon and cloves (optional)
250 gm (½ lb) sugar-candy
1 litre (2 pints) preserving brandy

Put the rind with the herbs in a bottle or jar and pour over the brandy. Cover closely and leave for 1 month. Filter off the brandy and add the sugar-candy. Put the lid back on the jar, and wait until the candy is full dissolved before you start drinking. You can shake the jar from time to time.

Variation Lemon Dutch gin can be made by substituting young Dutch gin for the brandy and by using much less sugar-candy.

Lemon Liqueur

rind of 4 lemons
rind of 1 orange
a few bruised coriander seeds
a clove
400 gm (14 oz) sugar
1 litre (2 pints) eau de vie or vodka

For preparation *see Lemon brandy.*

Variation Substitute cinnamon, mace and orange blossom for the clove and coriander.

Medlar *(Mespilus germanica)*

Small round fruits with a crown. Grey-green when fresh, brown when starting to decay. They can be kept in straw until fermentation has made them soft and you can suck the juice out.
Picking season not until the frost has got into them and they are soft and ripe.
Habitat cultivated, but still wild in some parts. A medlar tree or shrub in the garden used to be an excellent protection against the Devil and evil witches who feared it.

Medlars in eau de vie

Fill a wide-necked bottle or jar with the medlars into which you have pricked a few cloves. Weigh the medlars, sprinkle half their weight in sugar-candy over the top and fill the bottle up with eau de vie or cognac. Put the lid on tight. Leave for at least 2 months. This drink could also be combined with apples or pears.

Morello *(Prunus cerasus austera)*

A dark-red acid cherry with a strong flavour.
Picking season May–June
Habitat cultivated, especially on farms.
In former times it was also used in beer.

Morello ratafia

1 kilo (2 lbs) morellos
5 tsp mace
a clove
a piece of cinnamon stick
100 gm (3½ oz) sugar
1 litre (2 pints) brandy

Crush the morellos, pips and all, add the herbs and cover completely with brandy. Close securely and leave to soak for 4 weeks. Filter and add sugar. Shake from time to time until the sugar has dissolved. Can be served after only 2 months, but gets nicer if you wait for the tree to bloom again.

Morellos in brandy

1 kilo (2 lbs) morellos
450 gm (15½ oz) sugar-candy
a vanilla pod or
rind of an orange

Cut the stalks of the clean, dry morellos in

half and put the fruits in a preserving jar. Grind up the sugar-candy and sprinkle over the top. Pour over the brandy and put the lid on tight. Shake from time to time, until the candy is dissolved. This drink should not be served until the morello tree is in bloom once again.

Variation use Dutch gin instead of brandy and use less sugar-candy. Morellos are also very suitable in cognac.

East European Morello liqueur

Use a large preserving jar and fill with alternate layers of ripe red morellos (without stalks) and sugar. Do not fill it up completely. Cover the jar with a thin cloth and put it in a warm place. The contents will ferment and froth a little. Shake occasionally. When fermentation has come to an end, pour the liquid into a bottle (filtered if you like) and add ¼ litre (½ pint) of rectified spirit to each litre (2 pints) of liquid. Make sure the bottles are tightly closed and keep them in a dark place for 3 years, after which the liqueur is said to be at its best.

Mulberry *(Morus nigra)*

The fruit is a bit like blackberry
Picking season July–August
Habitat cultivated

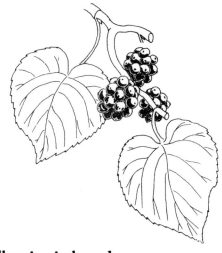

Mulberries in brandy

0.5 kilo (1 lb) mulberries
a piece of cinnamon stick
250 gm (½ lb) sugar
¾ litre (1½ pints) preserving brandy

Put all the ingredients together in a preserving jar or bottle and leave to mature for 3 months.

Mulberry liqueur

½ litre (1 pint) mulberry purée
a piece of cinnamon stick
a few cloves
a piece of vanilla pod
a piece of lemon rind
300 gm (9¾ oz) sugar
1 litre (2 pints) eau de vie

Let all the ingredients, except the sugar, macerate for 6 weeks. Then filter and add sugar, more or less according to taste. Leave to mature for another 6 weeks.

Orange *(Citrus aurantium sinensis)*

Oranges in brandy

1 kilo (2 pints) small oranges
150 gm (5 oz) sugar
1 litre (2 pints) brandy

Use preferably unsprayed oranges with thin rinds. Wash them well, rub them dry and cut, unpeeled, into thin slices. Remove the pips and put the slices in a preserving jar. Pour over brandy and cover the jar securely. Do not add sugar for a month. Shake occasionally and wait another month before serving.

Orange-coffee liqueur 'Quarante-quatre'

one very large orange
44 coffee beans
44 lumps sugar
half a vanilla pod
1 bottle eau de vie or cognac

Use the best, largest orange you can find, preferably with a thin rind and unsprayed. Wash it, rub it dry and with a knife make as many small cuts in it as possible. Stick the coffee beans in these cuts and put what is left in the bottom of a preserving bottle. Also add the orange with its 'bodice' of beans and the 44 lumps of sugar. Put in the vanilla and then the cognac or a good eau de vie. Let the drink mature for 44 days and filter.

Hanged man's orange liqueur

Use a very big, wide-necked preserving bottle, jar or bowl, and pour in a bottle of cognac, eau de vie or brandy. Add 250 gm (½ lb) of sugar. Take a nice big orange and hang it in the bottle on a string or in a piece of muslin, so that the fruit does not touch the surface of the alcohol. (The orange must not come into contact with the drink.) Close the bottle securely and leave the drink to mature for two months. Then remove the orange from the bottle and shake a few times if the sugar is not fully dissolved.

Clementine liqueur

For the preparation see *Oranges in Brandy*, but remove the clementine slices from the drink when it is ready. (Use them in a fruit salad.) The liqueur has to mature for a further month.

Eau de la belle alliance

rind of 2 oranges
3 tsp mace
200 gm (7 oz) sugar
¼ litre (½ pint) rosewater
¼ litre (½ pint) orange blossom water
½ litre (1 pint) rectified spirit

Let all the ingredients except the sugar soak for 6 weeks. Filter the drink and add the sugar. Bottle and leave to mature for another 6 weeks.

Peach *(Prunus persica)*

Picking season June–July
Habitat cultivated in sheltered sunny places

Peach leaf liqueur

Cut the young shoots of a peach tree into small pieces and fill half a preserving jar with them. Cover completely with eau de vie, put the lid on tight and leave to soak for 4 to 5 months. Then filter and add sugar to taste. As soon as the sugar is dissolved the liqueur is ready to serve.

Peaches in brandy

1 kilo (2 lbs) peaches
0.5 kilo (1 lb) sugar
¾ litre (1½ pints) brandy
a piece of orange rind (optional)

Cut the peaches in half, remove the stones and the skins. Crack the stones and take out the kernels. Make a sugar syrup with some water or wine and put the peaches and kernals in the syrup which should be hot but not boiling. Keep at the same temperature for 5 minutes, then take out the peaches and put them in a preserving jar. Leave the syrup to thicken a bit longer and then pour over the fruit. Cool and add the brandy. Close tightly and leave for 3 months.

Variation leave out the blanching (but the drink cannot be kept so long). You can also add ¼ litre (½ pint) of Persico.

Peach ratafia

0.75 kilo (1½ lb) peaches
a pinch of cinnamon
a pinch of cloves
a pinch of nutmeg
sugar to taste
1 bottle vodka

Cut the peaches, skin and all, into small pieces, crack the stones and chop up the kernels. Put the flesh, the kernels, cracked stones and herbs into a preserving jar, cover with a cloth and leave the mixture to soak for a few days. You can also pour the vodka over straight away and seal the jar. Let it stand for a month. Strain through a linen cloth and squeeze the juice out well. Add sugar to taste and when this is dissolved filter the liqueur. After a few months this liqueur is particularly good.

Eau de noyaux

Every time you eat peaches or apricots, keep the stones instead of throwing them away, crack them and chop up the kernels. Put the stones and kernels in a preserving jar and pour over a liberal amount of eau de vie or brandy. Repeat this until the jar is ¾ full, but make sure the jar is closed securely every time. The stones do not have to be absolutely clean, as this adds to the liqueur's bouquet. Let it mature for another 2 months, before filtering the drink and adding sugar to taste.

Shake from time to time until the sugar is dissolved.

Variation add a few skins of fruits which are in season, or rind of an orange, or some allspice.

Persico

250 gm (½ lb) peach stones
50 gm (2 oz) almonds
rind of a lemon
a few cloves
a piece of cinnamon stick
1 litre (2 pints) eau de vie or brandy
sugar to taste

Crack the stones and remove the kernels. Chop up the kernels and the almonds and put them in a preserving bottle, together with the cracked stones, the lemon rind and the herbs.
   Pour over the brandy or eau de vie and leave to soak for 6 weeks. Shake occasionally, add sugar and do not filter until it is dissolved. Bottle and leave for at least another 6 weeks.

Variation leave out the lemon rind and the cloves, and add a few cracked apricot stones with their chopped kernels, and 2 peppercorns. Or use brown sugar-candy instead of sugar.

Pear *(Pirus communis)*

Picking season September/October, except for a few varieties in August
Habitat cultivated

Pears in Rum

Peel the pears, remove the cores and cut them into pieces. Make a thick syrup with half the weight of the pears in sugar and a little water. Add the pear pieces, bring to the boil and gently simmer for 5 minutes. When they are cooled, cover them generously with rum. This drink will not keep indefinitely.

Pears in brandy

pears
some lemon juice and/or rind of a lemon
a piece of cinnamon stick
yellow or brown sugar-candy
brandy

For the preparation see *Pears in rum.*

Variation use eau de vie de poire instead of brandy for a change and leave out the lemon (juice and rind).

Pineapple *(Anarassa sativa)*

Can be bought fresh almost throughout the year.

Pineapple in eau de vie

Peel a fresh pineapple and cut the flesh into small pieces. Make sure that no peel is left on the pieces and discard the hard core. For each pound of fruit take 2 cloves and 150–200 gm (5–7 oz) of sugar. Half fill a preserving bottle or jar with the pineapple pieces, add the sugar and the cloves and top the bottle up with eau de vie. Close the container tightly and leave to mature for 3 to 4 months.

You can also filter the drink and use the pineapple in a fruit salad or other such dish.

Variation add ¼ litre (½ pint) of Kirsch, persico or cointreau. You can also use rum instead of eau de vie.

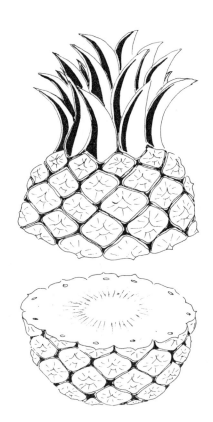

Pineapple liqueur

250 gm (½ lb) pineapple pulp
1 tsp saffron
½ pod vanilla
1 litre (2 pints) vodka

Mix all the ingredients together and let them soak for 14 days. Strain the drink through a cheesecloth and squeeze the pulp out well. Add sugar to taste and when dissolved filter the liqueur. Bottle and leave to mature for another few months.

Plum

The following varieties are mostly used in liqueur making: damsons *(Prunus domestica)*, the ordinary blue plums; Mirabelle plums, small, yellow-green round plums; Greengages, small green-yellow plums; Damast plums, early plums.
Picking season July/August
Habitat cultivated

Plums in cognac

0.75 kilo (1½ lb) greengages or mirabelles
300 gm (9¾ oz) sugar-candy
1 bottle cognac

Wash the plums, dry them carefully and prick them here and there with a silver fork (or darning needle). Put the plums in a preserving bottle or jar, sprinkle the crushed sugar-candy on top and cover everything with cognac. Make sure the bottle is securely closed and forget about it for 4 months.

Damast plums and gin

damast plums (damsons)
cloves to taste
almond essence
brown sugar or sugar-candy
dry London gin

For the preparation see *Plums in cognac.*

Plums in brandy

0.75 kilo (1½ lb) plums
a piece of cinnamon stick
a piece of lemon rind (optional)
350 gm (¾ lb) sugar
¾ litre (1½ pints) brandy

Wash the plums, dry them and prick them right through to the stone. Make a syrup by bringing the sugar, herbs and some water or wine to the boil, keep just off the boil for 5 minutes and cool. After 24 hours remove the plums from the syrup, put them in a jar or pot and reboil the syrup until it thickens. When cooled, pour over the plums and add the brandy. Make sure the bottle or jar is well-closed and store for a few months.

Variation add ¼ litre (½ pint) of Persico.

Prunes in armagnac

25 prunes
1 bottle armagnac

Put the prunes in a flask or bottle. Add the armagnac and close securely. You should not serve this drink until the prunes are fully swollen.

Variation use Slivovitz or another drink.

Prunes in eau de vie

Let the prunes soak in strong, sweet tea for 24 hours. Strain them and put them in a preserving bottle. Sprinkle brown sugar or sugar-candy on top (optional). Cover the prunes liberally with eau de vie and, if you like, add a piece of cinnamon stick and/or the rind of a lemon. A small stick of liquorice is also very nice. Close the bottle and let the drink mature for at least 2 months.

Pomegranate *(Punica granatum)*

A red-orange fruit with a leathery skin. Grenadine is made from this fruit.

Pomegranate liqueur

1 kilo (2 lbs) pomegranates
a piece of cinnamon stick
400 gm (14 oz) sugar
eau de vie

Use good, ripe, unblemished pomegranates. Cut them in half and remove the seeds. Make into a purée or liquidise them. Add cinnamon and eau de vie. Leave to mature in a well-closed jar for 4 weeks. Squeeze the purée through a cloth and add sugar. After the sugar is dissolved, filter and bottle the liqueur.

Eau de grenades (French pomegranate liqueur)

0.75 kilo (1½ lb) pomegranates
some orange blossom, dried
a piece of cinnamon stick
a blade of mace
a clove
400 gm (14 oz) sugar
1 litre (2 pints) vodka or eau de vie

For the preparation see *Pomegranate liqueur.*

Quince *(Cydonia vulgaris)*

A yellow pear-shaped fruit with a smooth skin.
Picking season September/October
Habitat only cultivated

Quince liqueur (as per French recipe)

Wash the quinces well and rub them dry. Peel them and put the skins in a preserving jar or pot. Add a good eau de vie and leave to macerate for about 6 weeks. Filter the liqueur and add about 350 gm (¾ lb) of sugar for each litre (2 pints) of liquid.

Excellent for stomach upsets, or so the French say.

Quince ratafia

Peel the quinces, grate them and press them through a cloth to get the juice out. Use the same amount of brandy as quince juice. Add 250 gm (½ lb) of sugar, 5 gm of cloves and 5 gm of cinnamon (both pulverised) for each litre (2 pints) of liquid. Leave in a dark place for 24 hours, until the sugar is dissolved. Pour through a filter and bottle.

Variation use only a few cloves, and add a few crushed almonds with some mace. Let this ratafia stand for 1 month. People sometimes used to add a few figs as well.

Eau de coings (a housewife's recipe from 1876)

25 sound quinces, finely grated
4 litres (8 pints) of brandy for each 4 litres (8 pints) of pulp
25 gm (1 oz) of loaf-sugar
90 gm (3½ oz) of almond paste
18 whole cloves
20 gm (¾ oz) of bruised coriander seeds

Must be allowed to soak for 8 days and then be filtered through paper.

Raisin

This is a dried grape.

Raisins in Brandy

An old Dutch drink which is still often made, especially in country areas. It used to be served at weddings in a large silver bowl or goblet, usually by the bride herself. They were called bride's tears. There are two explanations for these tears. One story goes that they were tears shed by the bride because she had to give up her parent's home, her maidenhood and her carefree youth for the uncertainties of married life. Another version is that they were tears of joy.

The raising of a glass was accompanied by the wish that these would be the last tears ever shed by the bride in her married life.

In other areas Ypocras (or hypocras, a spicy wine) was served as 'bride's tears'.

0.5 gm (1 lb) large seedless raisins
200 gm (7 oz) almonds
a stick of cinnamon
sugar-candy to taste
preserving brandy or
1 litre (2 pints) ordinary brandy

Put the raisins in a preserving jar. Blanch the almonds, peel them and chop them up. Add them to the raisins, along with the herbs, the sugar and the brandy. Close the jar securely and wait at least 2 weeks before serving the drink.

Variation first let the raisins soak in a sugar syrup for 24 hours. Add a piece of lemon or orange rind and a few cloves. Use Dutch gin or rum instead of brandy.

Raspberry *(Rubus Idaeus)*

A red fruit.
Picking season July
Habitat found here and there in the wild, in woods and in undergrowth, in open spaces and on the edges of woods. Also extensively cultivated.

Raspberries in Brandy

0.5 kilo (1 lb) raspberries
250 gm (½ lb) sugar
rind of 1 lemon or orange
½ vanilla pod (optional)
¾ litre (1½ pints) brandy

Carefully check the raspberries for grubs and blemishes. Put them in a jar, sprinkle sugar on top and add the herbs. Pour the brandy over the raspberries and put the lid on tight. After 1 month you will have a delicious drink.

Raspberry Liqueur I

0.5 kilo (1 lb) raspberries
300 gm (9¾ oz) sugar
a pinch of cinnamon
1 litre (2 pints) kirsch

For the preparation see *Raspberries in brandy*, but filter the liqueur after a month. Add some sugar (optional) and leave to mature for another 3 months.

Variation use brandy instead of kirsch and add vanilla, a few dried figs and 1/10 litre (⅓ pint) of rosewater.

Raspberry ratafia

0.5 kilo (1 lb) raspberries
250 gm (½ lb) cherries
350 gm (¾ lb) sugar
1 litre (2 pints) eau de vie

Carefully crush the washed cherries (fruit and pips) with a pestle and add the raspberries, which should also be squashed a little. Pour over the eau de vie and leave the mixture to soak for 2 weeks with the jar tightly closed. Then squeeze the pulp through a linen cloth to get as much juice as possible, and add sugar. Leave for another 14 days, then filter and bottle. Do not open this ratafia too soon.

Raspberry liqueur II

0.5 kilo (1 lb) raspberries
150 gm (5¼ oz) cherries
some mace
a piece of cinnamon stick
a few cloves
a piece of lemon rind
a piece of orange rind
300 gm (10 oz) sugar
1 bottle vodka

For the preparation see *Raspberry ratafia*.

Rose-hip *(Fructus cynosbati)*

The red fruit of the wild rose, also called dog rose
Picking season from August
Habitat in hedges, gardens, parks etc.
This very sweet-smelling fruit contains a lot of vitamin C and the liqueur is said to have a fortifying and stimulating effect (when taken in moderation: 3 times a day, 10–12 drops).

Rose-hip liqueur

400 gm (13¾ oz) rose-hips
sugar to taste
rind of an orange or lemon
a piece of cinnamon stick
1 litre (2 pints) eau de vie

Cut the rose-hips into pieces or bruise them, put the fruit in a bottle with the herbs and add the eau de vie. Leave to stand for 6 weeks, securely closed. Shake occasionally. Then filter, add sugar to taste and bottle. You can boil the fruit, rub it through a sieve and make it into a jelly.

Rowan Berry *(Sorbus aucuparia)*

An orange-red berry, from the mountain-ash. Has a harsh flavour.
Picking season not until after the first frost, but the birds usually beat you to it.
Habitat in woods.
When roasted, these berries can apparently be used as a coffee-substitute and are actually better than chicory and poor quality coffees.

Rowan berry ratafia

Thoroughly clean 0.5 kilo (1 lb) of rowan berries, put them in a bowl and mash them with a fork. Sprinkle 250 gm (½ lb) of sugar on top and stir into the mash. Put a cloth over the bowl and leave for a few days. Then add 1 litre (2 pints) of eau de vie and transfer to a preserving bottle or jar. Add a few herbs to taste, make sure the bottle is securely closed and leave for another month. Filter and add sugar to taste. Bottle.

Sloe *(Prunus spinosa)*

A small, dark blue, smooth fruit with a stone. Fruit of the blackthorn.
Picking season Just after the first frost
Habitat Found here and there in hedges and at the edges of fields

Sloe liqueur

0.5 kilo (1 lb) sloes
300 gm (10 oz) sugar
1 litre (2 pints) eau de vie

Prick the sloes with a darning needle or a silver fork. Put them in a jar, strew the sugar over them and cover with brandy. Shake daily for 3 months. Filter and bottle. Should really be left for another year. This liqueur is said to be a dream after 7 years.

Sloe gin

400 gm (14 oz) sloes
5 tsp bitter almonds
200 gm (7 oz) sugar
½ litre (1 pint) gin

For the preparation see *sloe liqueur*

Variation Leave out the almonds, but crush the sloes and grind up or crack the stones. You can also use sweet almonds instead of bitter ones.

Kayowsky

The sloes for this drink must be picked in September. Leave them in the sun for a day. Then remove the stones and crack them. Take 300 gm (9¾ oz) of the cracked stones, add a litre (2 pints) of eau de vie or vodka and leave to soak for 6 weeks, shaking daily. Then filter and add yellow or brown sugar-candy. Leave for another few months.

Strawberry *(Fragaria vesca)*

A soft red fruit
Picking season From May to June
Habitat These wild strawberries are much smaller but have more flavour than the cultivated ones and found extensively throughout Europe and North America. Cultivated strawberries can also be used.

Strawberries in brandy

0.5 kilo (1 lb) strawberries
250 gm (½ lb) sugar
½ litre (1 pint) brandy
vanilla and/or a piece of lemon rind (optional)

Put the clean strawberries in a jar and add the rest of the ingredients. After a month this drink is already delicious but will keep for longer—not *too* long, however.

Variation By lightly crushing the strawberries when putting them in the jar and sieving the drink after a month, you get a strawberry ratafia. This liqueur can be kept for longer than strawberries in brandy.

Ratafia of strawberries and raspberries

0.5 kilo (1 lb) sweet-smelling strawberries
300 gm (9¾ oz) raspberries
400 gm (13¾ oz) sugar
vanilla
a few coriander seeds
armagnac or eau de vie

Make a syrup of the sugar with some water by bringing to the boil and leaving to simmer for a while and aromatise with the vanilla and coriander. Pour the hot syrup over the fruit (which has been picked over but not washed) and leave the pulp, well covered, for 4 hours. Sieve the pulp, mix with old armagnac and bottle. (Or you can use eau de vie or half a litre (1 pint) of rectified spirit instead of armagnac.) Use the remaining fruit to make jam or bavarois.

According to Escoffier the above recipe for ratafia is better than any other. The flavour of the fruit is conserved better and the liqueur becomes fit to drink much sooner.

Strawberry liqueur with Sauterne

½ litre (1 pint) mashed strawberries or straw-berry purée
1 bottle Sauterne
sugar to taste
0.3 litre (⅔ pint) rectified spirit
a piece of lemon rind (optional)

Instead of Sauterne you can use another sweet white wine or home-made elderflower wine. Let the ingredients except the sugar stand for 2 weeks. Then filter and add sugar to taste. Drinkable after only a few weeks.

'Cordial water' by Sir Walter Raleigh from 1654

Put 4.5 litre (a gallon) of strawberries with 0.5 litre (1 pint) aqua vitae (brandy). Let it stand for 4 or 5 days. Sieve carefully. Sweeten this water with castor sugar and perfume according to taste.

Walnut *(Junglans regia)*

Picking season September–October
Habitat nowadays only found in old kitchen gardens
  This is because a walnut tree does not bear good fruit for 15–20 years and is not planted very often. Also, most mature trees have now been felled because of the value of the wood.
  Soft green nuts should be picked in July. The old book of *Ye Lady Jepheris* says the young nuts can best be gathered at the first full moon after midsummer night, but other days are also suitable.

Nuts in armagnac

Make a syrup by boiling a decilitre (¼ pint) of water or wine with 100 gm (3½ oz) sugar. Boil gently for ten minutes. Then add the

green nuts, pricked with a darning needle, and let them simmer gently for a little while. Put everything in a preserving bottle and fill up with armagnac. The nuts should be well covered. Let them stand for at least 2 months.

Brou de noix

12 new soft nuts
10 cloves
a whole nutmeg
250 gm (½ lb) sugar
1 litre (2 pints) eau de vie

Pound the nuts finely and put them in a preserving jar. Add the herbs and pour over the eau de vie. Leave to soak for 6 weeks. Sieve the drink through a cloth and squeeze out all the alcohol. Add the sugar and let the drink stand for another few weeks. Then filter and also decant, as a sediment is usually formed.

This drink is very good for the stomach: a few teaspoons full daily.

Nut liqueur I

12 soft green nuts
an orange
a piece of cinnamon stick
3 cloves
250 gm (½ lb) sugar
1 litre (2 pints) eau de vie

Chop the nuts into small pieces and put them in a preserving jar. Add the sliced orange (rind and all) as well as the herbs. Pour eau de vie over the nut mush, close the jar securely and leave to soak for 2-3 months. Filter the liqueur and add the sugar. Bottle. This drink should not be served until the sugar has completely dissolved. Mind you, the liqueur does become much nicer if you leave it for another year. The nuts can be boiled with some sugar and eaten as a compôte.

Variation add a piece of sweet flag to the herbs and use half brown and half white sugar.

Nut liqueur II

30 soft green walnuts
30 cloves
a piece of cinnamon stick
1½ tsp coriander
half a lemon
some mace (optional)
300–500 gm (10 oz–1 lb) sugar
1 litre (2 pints) vodka or brandy

For the preparation see *Nut liqueur 1*

Nuts in brandy

Take 50 fresh nuts, peel them and remove the skins. This is a fiddly job, but the skins are very bitter. Place the white pieces in a preserving bottle, add a vanilla pod split in half lengthwise and pour brandy over the mixture. Seal the bottle securely and let it stand for a few months. Then add sugar to taste and wait until the sugar has fully dissolved before serving the liqueur.

Nut liqueur III

10 fresh, moist walnuts with shells
a piece of cinnamon stick
a few cloves
honey
1 litre (2 pints) eau de vie

Crack the nuts and put them, shells and all, in the eau de vie together with the herbs. Leave to soak for a month. Then filter the drink and add honey to taste. Leave to mature for another few months.

Mixed fruit liqueurs

Eau de vie-pot
peach stones
blackcurrants
strawberries
raspberries
mulberries
morellos
etc.

Fill a large jar with a variety of fruits, eau de vie, cloves, cinnamon, and sugar candy and cover securely. Leave till the winter.

Guignolet d'Angers or red fruit ratafia

400 gm (13¾ oz) sour cherries (bird cherries)
200 gm (7 oz) morellos
100 gm (3½ oz) black cherries
100 gm (3½ oz) raspberries
80 gm (2¾ oz) red currants
40 gm (1¼ oz) blackcurrants
40 gm (1¼ oz) red carnations
2 tsp iris powder
1½ tsp cloves
1 tsp mace
1 tsp nutmeg
0.4 litre (1 pint) rectified spirit

Mash all the fruits and carnations together, cover the pulp with a cloth and leave for 2–3 days. Then add the herbs and the rectified spirit and leave to soak securely closed for a month. Strain the liquid through a cloth and squeeze the pulp well. Add sugar to taste (although the recipe says 50 gm (2 oz) you can use more or less). Let the liqueur mature for a further 2 months. Filter and bottle.

Ratafia ménagère

This liqueur is highly recommended in a French cookery book from 1807; it has a lovely bouquet and is highly suitable for the thrifty housewife.

Take a preserving bottle or jar, fill it up with eau de vie and daily add to this: peelings, cores, stones, fruits that are not good enough to serve fresh, left-overs from jam making, etc. The fruits and skins should be free from blemishes so cut these off. Close the bottle securely every time you top it up and make sure the mixture is always liberally covered with eau de vie. Also add some fragrant flowers or leaves to taste, and a few spices such as cinnamon, cloves and vanilla, if you like.

When the fruit season is over or when the bottle is full, strain the mixture through a cloth and squeeze it out well. Add sugar to taste and leave until Christmas. Filter and bottle. The ratafia can then be served immediately.

Rumpot

Start making this drink in early summer. Use a large preserving jar or a glazed crock which has a tight-fitting lid and place in it a thin layer of the first fruits of the season. Pour over as much rum as necessary to cover the fruits liberally, and close the jar. Throughout the season keep adding different fruits and some rum. Do not use too many watery fruits as this increases the risk of fermentation. Should this happen, add some rectified spirit. This hardly alters the flavour but stops fermentation. The fruits should be clean and dry and large fruits should be cut into pieces. When the season is over or when the jar is full, add sugar to taste.

Give this time to dissolve and you will have a beautiful drink, full of surprises.

There are many more fruit combinations to try, such as peaches and apricots; all kinds of citrus fruits with kirsch or rum; apples, pears and nuts; but I will leave this to your imagination.

Flower Liqueurs

These poetic liqueurs bring back sweet memories of sultry summer days gone by. So the flowers you use should preferably be picked and processed on a hot summer's day, 2 hours after sunrise. They must definitely not be sodden. Remove any damaged or brown petals and odourless parts such as the pistils, stamens and ovaries. Dried flowers can be bought at the chemist or health-food stores. Use these when you long for the summer and feel like making a flower liqueur. Dried flowers I have come across are orange blossom, violets, jasmin, lavender, verbena and roses. These flowers are obtainable in the form of tincture or oil, which are also highly suitable. Our ancestors made much use of this method of liqueur preparation.

There are many more flower liqueurs to consider than the ones I mention here. The only important thing is that the flowers should be heavily scented.

Carnation liqueur

Use the petals of the small red or wild carnation. Pick off as many petals as a preserving jar or bottle will hold and fill it up with brandy. Add a few cloves, a little cinnamon and/or mace but not too much in case they become overpowering. Cover the jar or bottle securely and leave for 6 weeks. Then filter and add sugar to taste. Leave for at least another 3 weeks. Shake now and again, though. The French consider this liqueur excellent for indigestion.

Lavender liqueur

150 gm (5 oz) lavender flowers
3 tsp aniseed
3 tsp paradise seed or peppercorns
1 litre (2 pints) brandy
350 gm (¾ lb) sugar

Put the flowers, herbs and brandy in a preserving jar or bottle and let them stand for 6 weeks. Then filter and add sugar. Shake now and then until the sugar is completely dissolved.

Jasmine liqueur

Very early in the morning add 400 gm (14 oz) of sugar to ½ litre (1 pint) water and bring to the boil. As soon as the syrup starts boiling add 200 gm (7 oz) of jasmine petals, preferably with the morning dew still on them and immediately remove from the heat. Leave to soak well-covered for another 15 minutes. When the jasmine syrup is completely cool pour it into a preserving bottle and add 1 litre (2 pints) of eau de vie. Close tightly and leave to mature for 6 weeks. Then filter and keep in a cool, dark place.

Poppy liqueur (about 1840) *'Swift Water' according to Queen Victoria*

Take 3 poppies from a cornfield and put them in a litre (2 pints) of brandy. Leave to soak for 2 days and nights, then pick them out and add to the brandy:

100 gm (3½ oz) sugar
200 gm (7 oz) seedless raisins
12 gm (½ oz) top quality licorice, scraped and sliced
3 tsp aniseed, bruised
3 tsp Venetian syrup
1½ tsp saffron, dried and finely ground
⅛ litre (¼ pint) primrose water
1 flat tsp long pepper, bruised
1 flat tsp virginia snake-root *(Calla palustris)*
1 flat tsp cardamom

Add these all together and leave them in a

glass jar in the sunshine for 3 weeks. Shake once a day. Filter before use.

May blossom liqueur (about 1775)

Try to gather the may blossom (of the hawthorn) on a dry, calm day when there is no dust flying about. Pick as much as a preserving jar will hold. Fill it up with brandy or eau de vie. Close the jar and shake it 3 times a week for 3 months. Filter and if necessary add sugar to taste. Excellent in custards and sauces.

Orange blossom liqueur

As *'carnation liqueur'*. Or use 100 gm (3½ oz) of dried orange blossom.

Eau de Fleur d'orange

100 gm (3½ oz) orange blossom, dried
10 tsp red roses, dried
2 tsp lemon balm
2 tsp thyme
2 tsp aniseed
1½ tsp cinnamon
6 tsp orange rind
1 litre (2 pints) brandy or eau de vie
350 gm (¾ lb) sugar

Add the flowers and herbs to the brandy and leave the mixture to soak for 6 weeks. Then filter and add sugar. This liqueur is rather spicy for our tastes; you can safely use fewer herbs.

Rosolio

50 gm (1¾ oz) crown leaves of a heavily-scented rose
25 gm (1 oz) desiccated currants
3 flat tsp jasmine flowers
2 pinches cinnamon
2 pinches mace
1 pinch cloves
¾ litre (1½ pints) brandy
200 gm (7 oz) sugar

Mix everything together except the sugar and leave to stand for a month. Then strain through a cloth or filter and add the sugar. Leave for a while longer.

Rossolis from France

80 gm (2¾ oz) nutmeg roses
50 gm (1¾ oz) orange blossom
25 gm (1 oz) jasmine blossom
1½ tsp cinnamon
½ tsp cloves
1 litre (2 pints) eau de vie
sugar

Mix everything together except the sugar and leave to soak for a month. Filter or squeeze through a cloth and add the sugar. The drink will benefit from storing for a few months in cool dark place.

Rossolis de mille fleurs

35 gm (1¼ oz) sweet-smelling red roses
10 gm (½ oz) jasmine flowers
10 gm (½ oz) orange blossom
5 gm (¼ oz) lavender flowers
5 gm (¼ oz) rosemary flowers
small handful heliotrope flowers
small handful mignonette flowers
1½ tsp cinnamon
1½ tsp mace
1 litre (2 pints) eau de vie or brandy
sugar

Let all the ingredients, except the sugar, soak together for a month. Squeeze the mixture through a cloth or pour it through a filter and add sugar to taste. Put the drink, securely covered, in a cool dark place and shake now and then until the sugar has dissolved.

Rossolis from Turin

60 gm (2 oz) sweet-smelling roses
50 gm (1¾ oz) jasmine flowers
50 gm (1¾ oz) orange blossom
10 gm (½ oz) cinnamon
1½ tsp cloves
2 tsp mace
a piece of lemon rind
1 litre (2 pints) brandy
sugar

Put all the ingredients together in a preserving jar or bottle and leave to soak for a month. Filter and add sugar to taste. You can also give the liqueur a nice purple or dark red colour.

Eau verveine

Use verbena or vervain in the same way as 'Carnation liqueur'.

Elder blossom liqueur

Use the whole umbels and follow the same method as for 'Jasmine liqueur'.

Violet liqueur

75 gm (2¾ oz) fresh violets
25 gm (1 oz) iris powder
1 tsp aniseed
1 tsp cinnamon
½ tsp cloves
a piece of orange rind
1 litre (2 pints) brandy
sugar

Deep purple violets are the tastiest. Make sure you choose a sweet-smelling variety. Put everything, except the sugar, in a preserving jar and leave to soak for a month. Then filter, add sugar to taste and colouring if you like.

Violet liqueur without flowers

30 gm (1¼ oz) iris powder
50 gm (1¾ oz) litmus powder
a piece of lemon rind
1 litre (2 pints) brandy

Let all the ingredients, except the sugar, macerate for a few days. Filter the solution and add the sugar. In spite of the absence of violets this liqueur gives off a pleasant violet-like scent. Iris powder is in fact also called violet root.

Herb Liqueurs and Bitters

There are many different versions of some famous herb liqueurs. I found 17 recipes for *Vespetro*, 12 for *Parfait-amour* and at least 10 for *Curaçao*. From this is seems obvious that you can easily concoct your own *Vespetro* or *Eau de ma tante*, just as our ancestors did.

The herbs can be used either fresh or dried. The dried herbs especially should be of a good quality and should have retained as much of their aroma as possible. Old and musty herbs are the very devil. The best extracts are obtained by crushing the seeds, chopping the roots up into small pieces, as well as the fresh herbs, figs and bark. You can also grind the aromatic ingredients, in your coffee-mill for example. The kind of alcoholic base you use is not so important, because the flavour of the herbs is usually predominant.

Basic recipe

Let the herbs and spices soak in the alcohol for at least 4 to 6 weeks. Use a distilled drink such as brandy, eau de vie, vodka or some other drink, or extract the herbs in ½ litre (1 pint) of rectified spirit (see *Advice* under alcohol). Make sure you use a bottle or pot which can be closed securely and put it in a moderately warm place. After extraction filter the drink and add sugar. If you have used rectified spirit first make a syrup of the sugar and ½ litre (1 pint) of water, and when cooled pour it onto the drink. Bottle, and preferably leave to mature for another 6 months or so in a cool dark place.

Absinth

15 gm (⅔ oz) wormwood
2½ tsp aniseed
2½ tsp cinnamon
1 or 2 cloves
1 litre (2 pints) eau de vie
350–500 gm (¾–1 lb) sugar

For preparation see Basic recipe.

Angelica liqueur

25 gm (1 oz) angelica
2½ tsp cinnamon
2 flat tsp coriander
2 flat tsp aniseed
1 flat tsp mace
a piece of lemon rind
1 litre (2 pints) eau de vie
350–500 gm (¾–1 lb) sugar

For preparation see Basic recipe.

Liqueur des anges

50 gm (1¾ oz) angelica root
½ tsp cinnamon
½ tsp nutmeg
1 litre (2 pints) eau de vie
0.5 kilo (1 lb) sugar

For preparation see Basic recipe.

Anisette

10 gm (5 tsp) aniseed
1¼ tsp coriander
¾ tsp cinnamon
¾ tsp nutmeg
1 litre (2 pints) brandy
350 gm (¾ lb) sugar

For preparation see Basic recipe.

Anisette de Bordeaux

3 tsp aniseed
2 tsp star anise
¾ tsp coriander
¾ tsp fennel
1 litre (2 pints) eau de vie
450 gm (15½ oz) sugar

For preparation see Basic recipe.

Anti-humdrum liqueur

40 twigs fresh savoury
2 cloves
split vanilla pod
1 litre (2 pints) brandy
50 gm (1¾ oz) sugar

For preparation see Basic recipe.

Basque liqueur

4 flat tsp coriander
4 flat tsp bitter almonds
1½ tsp angelica root
½ tsp cardamom
1 litre (2 pints) eau de vie
300 gm (10 oz) sugar

For preparation see Basic recipe.

Chartreuse (imitation)

1½ tsp angelica
1 tsp balm
1 tsp mint
1¼ tsp hyssop
½ tsp aniseed
¼ tsp coriander
1 tsp fir-tree buds
1 litre (2 pints) brandy
375 gm (13 oz) sugar
a little green colouring

For preparation see Basic recipe.

Chartreuse-like liqueur

¼ tsp saffron
13 whole cardamoms
rind of 2 lemons
400 gm (10 oz) sugar
1 litre (2 pints) brandy

Remove the seeds from the cardamoms and
see Basic recipe for preparation.

Coffee liqueur

60 gm (2 oz) ground coffee
a little vanilla and/or cocoa (optional)
1 litre (2 pints) eau de vie
250 gm (½ lb) sugar

For preparation see Basic recipe. This liqueur
only has to mature for 14 days. Instead of eau
de vie you could use another drink, such as
whisky or rum. If you like the combination,
you can add some peppermint or a few pieces
of orange rind.

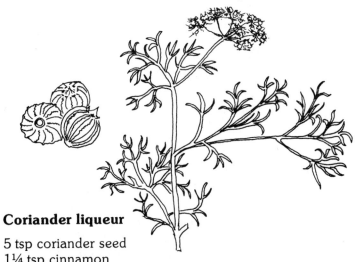

Coriander liqueur

5 tsp coriander seed
1¼ tsp cinnamon
a few cloves
a few juniper berries
1 litre (2 pints) brandy or vieux
150 gm (5¼ oz) sugar

For preparation see Basic recipe.

Crème de cacao

30 gm (1¼ oz) cocoa
½ tsp vanilla
a piece of lemon rind
1 litre (2 pints) vodka
450 gm (15½ oz) sugar

For preparation see Basic recipe.

Curaçao I

35 gm (1¼ oz) bitter orange rind
1 tsp cinnamon
½ oz mace
1 litre (2 pints) eau de vie
400 gm (13¾ oz) sugar

The orange rind should be lightly toasted. For further preparation see Basic recipe.

Curaçao II

Take the rinds of 3 oranges and toast them in the oven until they are light brown. When they have cooled off put them in a litre of rum and let them soak for 6 weeks. Then make a sugar syrup of 350 gm (¾ lb) of sugar and a little water, add the rinds of 3 fresh oranges and simmer for a while. Cool and pour into the alcohol. Leave to soak for another 6 weeks, then filter and bottle. You can also add a little almond essence and/or cloves, mace and cinnamon.

Dill liqueur

20 gm (1 oz) dill leaves and stems
20 gm (1 oz) fennel leaves and stems
20 gm (1 oz) anise leaves
1 litre (2 pints) brandy
250 gm (½ lb) sugar

For preparation see Basic recipe.

Honey liqueur

10 gm (⅓ oz) peppermint herb
1¼ tsp thyme
1¼ tsp hyssop
1 litre (2 pints) rum
250 gm (½ lb) honey

Let the herbs soak in the alcohol for a week. Filter and add the honey, bottle and shake from time to time to let the honey dissolve.

Izarra liqueur

15 gm (½ oz) iris powder
3½ tsp coriander
3½ tsp aniseed
1 litre (2 pints) eau de vie
350 gm (¾ lb) sugar

For preparation see Basic recipe.

Juniper berry liqueur

16 gm (½ oz) juniper berries
2 gm (1 tsp) star anise
3 gm(1½ tsp) coriander
2 gm (1 tsp) cinnamon
2 gm (1 tsp) paradise seed
lemon rind (optional)
1 litre (2 pints) brandy
250 gm (½ lb) sugar

For preparation see Basic recipe.

Kümmel liqueur

25 gm (1 oz) caraway
1 tsp iris powder
½ tsp aniseed
½ tsp coriander
a few petals chamomile blossom
2 pinches lemon rind, grated
1 litre (2 pints) vodka
sugar to taste

For preparation see Basic recipe. If you want a liqueur with sugar crystals then see *Advice*, under sweetenings.

Variation leave out all the herbs except caraway.

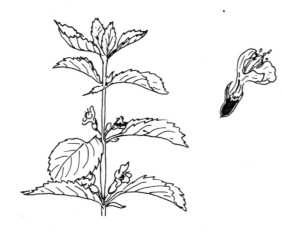

Lemon Balm liqueur

100 gm (3½ oz) lemon balm
2½ tsp cinnamon
1½ tsp cloves
¾ tsp nutmeg
5 tsp lemon rind grated
1 litre (2 pints) eau de vie
200 gm (7 oz) sugar

For preparation see Basic recipe.

Liqueur du Prince d'Orange

40 gm (1½ oz) apricot stones
10 gm (⅓ oz) angelica seed
10 gm (⅓ oz) angelica root
2½ tsp cinnamon
⅓ tsp vanilla
3 tsp orange blossom
1 litre (2 pints) brandy
350 gm (¾ lb) sugar

For preparation see Basic recipe.

Mint liqueur

100 gm (3½ oz) mint
100 gm (3½ oz) peppered spirit of mint
1 handful orange blossom
1 litre (2 pints) brandy
350 gm (¾ lb) sugar

For preparation see Basic recipe.

Parfait-amour I

1½ tsp coriander
½ tsp cinnamon
½ tsp mace
a few cloves
1½ tsp iris powder
2 tsp bitter almonds
a piece of lemon rind
1 litre (2 pints) eau de vie
0.5 kilo (1 lb) sugar

For preparation see Basic recipe. This liqueur can be given an amethyst colour by mixing together red and blue.

Parfait-amour II

4 gm (2 tsp) vanilla
4 gm (2 tsp) rosemary
1 gm (½ tsp) cinnamon
4 gm (2 tsp) orange blossom
a few cloves
0.5 gm (¼ tsp) mace
1 gm (½ tsp) cardamom
rind of 1 lemon
1 litre (2 pints) brandy
250 gm (½ lb) sugar

For preparation see Basic recipe. This liqueur
can be coloured yellow with 1 gm of saffron
or, like the previous one, amethyst. You can
also colour it red.

Peppermint liqueur

25 gm (1 oz) peppermint herb
a few cloves
some mace
some orange blossom
20 gm (¾ oz) lemon rind
1 litre (2 pints) brandy
250 gm (½ lb) sugar

For preparation see Basic recipe. This liqueur
is usually coloured green.

Variation leave out all the herbs except
peppermint.

Persico

100 gm (3½ oz) apricot kernels
50 gm (1¾ oz) peach kernels
5 tsp orange blossom
a few leaves lemon balm
1 tsp mace
1 tsp cinnamon
4 cloves
10 gm (5 tsp) lemon rind
1 litre (2 pints) brandy
300 gm (10 oz) sugar, brown

For preparation see Basic recipe.

Rosemary liqueur

20 gm (¾ oz) fresh rosemary
3 tsp lavender
2½ tsp marjoram
2½ tsp thyme
1 tsp tailed pepper or pepper
1½ tsp cardamom
1 litre (2 pints) brandy
sugar to taste

For preparation see Basic recipe.

Scubac

1¼ tsp saffron
1½ tsp juniper berries
½ tsp aniseed
½ tsp coriander
1¼ tsp cinnamon
2 cloves
¼ tsp mace
½ tsp angelica root
a few jujubes (optional)
1 litre (2 pints) eau de vie
250 gm (½ lb) sugar

For preparation see Basic recipe.

Steernties

12 gm (½ oz) star-anise
5 twigs saffron
1 litre (2 pints) brandy
350 gm (¾ lb) sugar

For preparation see Basic recipe. You can also add a little cardamom and half vieux, half brandy.

Tea liqueur

Make a concentrated pot of tea from 125 gm (4½ oz) of aromatic tea and ¼ litre (½ pint) of hot water. When cooled, add ¼ litre (½ pint) of rectified spirit and ¼ litre (½ pint) of rum, as well as 125 gm (4½ oz) of sugar or honey. Close the bottle and leave in daylight for a month.

Add some lemon rind if necessary.

Usquebac from Ireland

rind of ⅔ orange
rind of 1 lemon
a vanilla pod
1½ tsp mace
5 gm (2 tsp) cloves
1½ tsp angelica
¾ tsp sugar root (chicory)
¾ tsp coriander
2 tsp saffron
1 litre (2 pints) brandy
400 gm (14 oz) sugar

For preparation see Basic recipe.

Vanilla liqueur

Add a vanilla pod, split lengthwise, and 125 gm (4½ oz) of sugar to ¼ oz litre (½ pint) of water, bring to the boil and simmer for 10 minutes. Let it cool and then add ¼ litre (½ pint) of rectified spirit (see *Advice* under alcohol) and ½ litre (1 pint) of rum. Leave to soak for 14 days. Filter and bottle. If you like, you can add cinnamon, nutmeg or lemon rind.

Crème de vanille

0.5 kilo (1 lb) icing sugar
½ vanilla pod
juice of 2 lemons
½ litre (1 pint) milk
½ litre (1 pint) rectified spirit

Vespetro II

2½ tsp green tea
10 gm (⅓ oz) apricot kernels
4 tsp fennel
3 tsp lemon rind
2½ tsp orange rind
2½ tsp star-anise
2½ tsp coriander
2½ tsp angelica root
1 litre (2 pints) brandy
350 gm (¾ lb) sugar

For preparation see Basic recipe. Celery seed, caraway, dill, musk etc. can also be added.

For rectified spirit see *Advice* under alcohol. Mix the icing sugar and the lemon juice together and stir until the sugar is fully dissolved. Mix in the rectified spirit and the milk and add the vanilla pod. Put the drink in a clear bottle, close tightly and leave on the window-sill for 8–14 days. Then filter and bottle. The crème can be served after only a few weeks, but the flavour improves noticeably by the month.

Vespetro I (the authentic)

20 gm (⅔ oz) angelica root
20 gm (⅔ oz) coriander
20 gm (⅔ oz) star anise
20 gm (⅔ oz) fennel
1 litre (2 pints) brandy
250 gm (½ lb) sugar
a little lemon and orange rind (optional)

For preparation see Basic recipe.

Bitters

Angostura bitter

5 gm (2½ tsp) gentian root
5 gm (2½ tsp) galangal root
5 gm (2½ tsp) angostura bark
7 gm (3½ tsp) cardamom
7 gm (3½ tsp) cinnamon
1 gm (½ tsp) angelica
1 gm (½ tsp) ginger root
4 cloves
7 gm (3½ tsp) bitter orange rind
17 gm (⅔ oz) sandalwood
17 gm (⅔ oz) tonquin beans
1 litre (2 pints) vieux or brandy
50 gm (1¾ oz) sugar

For preparation see Basic recipe, but the herbs do not have to soak for more than 14 days.

Berenburger-like bitter

50 gm (1¾ oz) sweet flag
50 gm (1¾ oz) bogbean
2½ tsp small coltsfoot
2½ tsp blessed thistle
2½ tsp sandalwood
2½ tsp gentian root
2½ tsp juniper berries
2½ tsp bay berry
1 litre (2 pints) Dutch gin

Let the herbs soak in the Dutch gin for 3 weeks. Filter and add Dutch gin to taste. You can also use brandy.

Dutch bitters

20 gm (⅔ oz) bitter orange rind
10 gm (⅓ oz) juniper berries
15 gm (½ oz) gentian root
2 tsp elecampane root
5 gm (1/6 oz) quinine
1 litre (2 pints) brandy

Toast the bitter orange rind in the oven until it is golden brown. For further preparation see Basic recipe. You can add 200 gm (7 oz) of sugar, if you like.

English bitters

1¼ tsp sweet flag
½ tsp ginger root
10 gm (⅓ oz) gentian root
½ tsp elecampane root
½ tsp cinnamon
rind of ½ lemon
rind of ½ orange
1 litre (2 pints) gin or brandy

For preparation see Basic recipe. You can add sugar if you like.

Gentian bitters

20 gm (⅔ oz) gentian root
5 gm (1/6 oz) blessed thistle
5 gm (1/6 oz) lemon balm
1½ tsp aniseed
1 tsp cinnamon

For preparation see Basic recipe. Add sugar if you like.

Highland bitters

25 gm (1 oz) gentian root
3½ tsp bitter orange rind
15 gm (⅔ oz) coriander
a handful chamomile flowers
cinnamon stick
3 tsp cloves
1 litre (2 pints) whisky
sugar to taste, (optional)

For preparation see Basic recipe.

Love Potions

Nearly every civilisation has, at one time or another, ascribed a love-stimulating effect to certain herbs. In certain Asian countries and in the Middle East they have always concocted the most fantastic love potions which sometimes use alcohol to heighten the effect, and a sweetener to make the taste more agreeable. When taken in very large amounts, some herbs indeed seem to arouse passionate feelings. In the Middle Ages people had a firm belief in the power of love-potions, usually prepared by sorceresses. The best were the so-called white witches, with their exclusively benevolent magic, but you could also go to the black (evil) witches for a love-potion. Both had a cupboardful of mixtures which ranged from completely innocuous remedies for general use down to vile elixirs and deadly poisons.

Very many popular tales and legends mention love-potions, and the most famous of these is the story of Tristan and Isolde. Because, by accident, Tristan has a magic potion put before him and drinks it, he falls in love with Isolde who belongs to someone else.

The power of the magic drink is so great that even death cannot part them.

In the time of Louis XIV the administration of love-potions was still thought an excellent way to arouse or retain desire. Those who could afford it went to the dreaded and notorious sorceress Catherine La Voisin. She was an expert on herbs and potions, was a midwife, prophesied the future and practised black magic. Even the king's mistress used to go to her for love-potions, and the great occasion (l'affair des Poisons) that people wanted to make of the execution of this woman and her accomplices was hushed up by Louis XIV himself, when he saw Madame de Montespan's name on the list of her clients.

Nowadays people's faith in love-potions has by and large disappeared, but I will not withold a number of recipes from you in case you would like to try them. The most important herbs that traditionally qualify as aphrodisiacs are: dill, sweet flag, cinnamon, cardamom, caraway, coriander, lovage, nutmeg and celery.

Lovage

100 gm (3½ oz) freshly chopped celery root
3 tsp fennel seed
½ tsp cinnamon
3½ tsp caraway
1 litre (2 pints) gin
100 gm (3½ oz) sugar

Let the herbs soak in the gin for 14 days. Filter the drink and add sugar to taste. A long maturation time will definitely increase the magic effect.

Philtre magique

20 gm (¾ oz) cinnamon
a small handful of rose petals
1 small handful nutmeg
1 litre (2 pints) eau de vie
sugar-candy

Let the herbs and the rose-petals macerate in the eau de vie for 14 days. Filter the drink and add sugar. The drink should be left to mature for another few months to develop fully.

Farmer's love-potion

8 gm (4 tsp) fennel seed
6 gm (3 tsp) celery seed
6 gm (3 tsp) angelica
5 gm (2½ tsp) coriander seed
1 litre (2 pints) brandy
sugar

Let the herbs, which you must crush or grind, soak in the brandy for 14 days. Then filter the liquid and add sugar to taste. The story goes that, just like the farmer's love, this drink needs time to blossom.

Venus liqueur

12.5 gm (½ oz) carrot seed
5 gm (2½ tsp) cinnamon
7.5 gm (3½ tsp) caraway
1.5 gm (¾ tsp) mace
0.5 gm (¼ tsp) saffron
1 litre (2 pints) eau de vie
350 gm (¾ lb) sugar

Let the herbs macerate in the alcohol for at least 14 days. Then filter the drink and add sugar to taste. The liqueur now has to be left to mature for some time. Instead of eau de vie you can use another kind of alcohol and instead of using saffron you could colour the liqueur rose-red with cochineal. Even the proportions of herbs are unimportant as they change from one author to the next.

Love-potion

Take any nice liqueur and add some cantharides (a South-European beetle, which has been dried and ground to powder). It is better known under the name *Spanish Fly* and according to the Marquis De Sade, success is assured with it. He apparently put this in delicious chocolates and then presented them at a ball. The ball ended in a real orgy.

Love-potion for older men

As the moon is rising, soak 300 gm (9¾ oz) of fresh, chopped-up truffles in 2 litres (4 pints) of old bourgogne. On the third day after full moon take 12 crayfish and boil them for 20 minutes in a stock which you have made from pepper, caraway, anise, thyme, red peppers and a celery stalk. Rub the ingredients through a sieve to produce a fluid purée and let this thicken *au bain-marie* for 24 hours. Then press through a cloth, add the chopped-up testicles of a 2 year old white cockerel and leave to macerate for 3 hours. Then add the bourgogne and a litre (2 pints) of 80% eau de vie. Leave your liqueur, well-covered, to soak for a whole night. Sieve and filter once again and finally add a bouquet of freshly picked alum blossom and soak for 75 minutes. A glass of this for the woman of your dreams, a glass of this for you, and you will see . . .

Apparently this is the drink to which Tristan's love for Isolde is ascribed.

Liber de arte Distil
landi de Compositis.

Das büch der waren kunst zü distillieren die

Composita vñ simplicia/vnd dz Büch thesaurus pauperu̅/Ein schatz 8 arme̅ ge)
nāt Vicariū/die bröslamlin gefallen vo̅ de̅ büchern 8 Artzny/vnd durch Experime̅t
vo̅ mir Jheronimo beu̅schwick vff geclu̅bt vñ geoffenbart zü trost dene̅ die es begere̅.

getruckt un gendigt in die keisserliche frye statt Strassburg
uff sanct Mathis abent in dem jar 1507.

Medicinal liqueurs and elixirs

For centuries people have been convinced that distilled alcohol has healing properties. In the Middle Ages brandy was still only sold as a medicine and was taken in minute quantities. During the many epidemics that dominated the 14th century (like the *Black Death*, which raged from 1340–1350) big money was asked—and paid—for a few drops of this valuable liquid. Physicians from those times were in fact quick to recommend brandy, because they considered that the feeling of warmth it created in the body was the best guard against typhoid, diarrhoea and the like.

One of the most famous songs in praise of the virtues of alcohol is by the Strassburger doctor Hieronymus Brunschwig (1450–1534, also called Braunschweig, Brunschwygk or Brunschwijg). This giant in the field of medical science, surgery and pharmacology in 15th century Germany described aqua vitae as follows:

'Aqua vitae is the mistress of all medicines. It alleviates illnesses caused by the cold. It refreshes the heart. It cures all old and new headaches. It gives people a good colour. It cures baldness, makes the hair grow well and kills lice and fleas. It cures lethargy. A few pieces of cotton wool, dipped into it, squeezed out and put in the ears, together with drinking a little of it in the evening just before going to bed, is good for deafness. It relieves toothache and sweetens the breath. It cures cancer of the teeth, lips and tongue, if it is kept in the mouth. It makes a poor speaker eloquent. It cures shortness of breath. It produces good digestion and appetite and takes away flatulence. It extracts wind from the body. It relieves yellow fever, dropsy, gout, pain in the breasts when they are swollen, heals bladder complaints and breaks the stones.

It draws out poison which has been taken in meat or drinks if a little syrup is added. It heals all shrivelled nerves and makes them soft and straight. It cures fever that has lasted for two or three days. It cures the bites of a mad dog as well as all stinking wounds if they are washed with it. It gives people fresh courage and a good memory. It clears the five senses of melancholy and of all impurities.' But it should be taken in moderation and sensibly, warned Brunschwig: this would mean 5 to 6 drops in the morning with a spoonful of wine at breakfast. From which we may justifiably conclude that over-indulgence existed from very early on.

In the Middle Ages and Renaissance people started adding more and more herbs and spices to brandy and the preparation of liqueurs was then mainly in the hands of apothecaries, usually monks, the most important herb connoisseurs in those days.

Herbs and spices played a very important role, not only in liqueurs, but also in the medieval kitchen. They had to be brought from afar, though, and were very expensive and scarce. This is apparent from the welcoming gesture (considered extremely benevolent and hospitable) which a town-council had to make when royalty was visiting. The dignitary would be offered a few boxes of *cruyt* or a spiced cake as a present. Naturally these cakes were not made from native herbs, but from spices like cinnamon, pepper, cardamon and sugar, for sugar too, was scarce and could be bought from an apothecary. The combination of herbs and brandy made liqueur into a truly miraculous remedy (panacée or allheilmittel) and all kinds of herbs were used very lavishly, probably because people thought: the dearer, the better! An example of a drink, or rather elixir, for which no cost nor trouble were spared, is the following from about 1730:

Add to 8 stoops (8 x 2.5 litre) of brandy:

20 gm of Caliga
12½ gm of cubeba
10 gm of bayleaves
10½ gm of zedoary roots
20 gm of small cardamom seeds
20 gm of gentian roots
20 gm of Rhaponticum or wild rhubarb
20 gm of angelica
20 gm of chamomile
20 gm of sweet flag
20 gm of lemon rind
20 gm of fennel seed
20 gm of carrot seed
20 gm of liquorice
20 gm of cardamom
20 gm of aniseed
half a quarter of ginger
20 gm of nutmeg
20 gm of cinnamon
20 gm of mace
10 gm of cloves
20 gm of sage
a handful of common rue
a handful of juniper berries
To sweeten, add 0.75 kilo of best sugar, and just over a 'mengelen' (1.53 litre) of rainwater. To colour add 125 gm of sandalwood to one can (about 1 litre).

Gold-leaf and silver-leaf were also added to liqueurs for their assumed medicinal and life-prolonging properties. They can still be found in one or two drinks as decoration.

During the 17th and 18th centuries people in France were very fond of cassis (blackcurrant liqueur), to which at least a thousand-and-one good virtues have been ascribed. It even surpassed balsam of Peru, and people claimed that mortally ill horses, for which all other remedies known at the time had failed, were cured by cassis.

The well-known Dutch physician Cornelius Bontekoe in 1750 prescribed an antiscorbutic or scurvy liqueur. He used mace, nutmeg, cloves, lemon or orange rind, soaked all these in brandy and sweetened it with sugar. The vitamin C from the rind is indeed a good remedy against scurvy.

In *Secrets of Wines*, 1730, all kinds of curative waters can be found (based on brandy, not on water) such as:
  true Lung-Water
  Breast-Water
  Rupture-Water
  Stomach-Water and For a chill on the Stomach
  Plague-Water and good Plague-Water
  delicious Mouth-Water
  Wind-Water
In the names of other old liqueurs the curative effect is also expressed:
'Maternity anise' which benefited the womb and the woman's milk glands.
'Shirt-lifter' as a purgative for constipation.
Venus oil (*Huile de Venus* of the Frenchman Sigogne who made a fortune from it) for its aphrodisiac effect. And the 'Cordial' created by the Genevan apothecary Coladon, for its excellent influence on the heart.

But even today old uses of brandy can still be found. It once happened to me that when I complained to my hairdresser about my hair falling out, he recommended that I should rub ordinary brandy or gin into my hair every night. I faithfully did this with a whole bottleful (although a few glasses of it disappeared into my stomach, but not many, honestly) but to my disappointment it has no effect whatsoever. However, the hairdresser had actually noticed an improvement of hair growth in some customers, as a result of the application of alcohol.

I would not venture to guarantee the actual curative influence of the following recipes, but there are people who have benefited from them.

Against colics

0.5 kilo (1 lb) blackcurrants
2 tsp cinnamon
1 tsp cloves
½ tsp coriander
1 litre (2 pints) brandy

Pound the ripe fruits thoroughly and mix them with the rest of the ingredients. After soaking for 14 days squeeze out well, filter and add 375 gm (13 oz) or less of sugar, to taste.

Fever bitters (for ordinary 2 or 3 day fevers)

25 gm (1 oz) best brown Quinine or Peruvian bark
12 gm (½ oz) finely sliced Curaçao rind

12 gm (½ oz) peppermint herb (powerful and not old)
12 gm (½ oz) wormwood buds
3 tsp finely chopped gentian root
3 tsp finely chopped sweet flag root
2 tsp blessed thistle
2 tsp centaury
2 tsp juniper berries
1 litre (2 pints) Dutch gin

Put all the ingredients together in a bottle and cover securely. Put the bottle in a cool dark place and leave the mixture to soak for 2 months. Make sure you shake it daily. Then filter and squeeze the herbs well. 2, 3 or up to 6 spoonfuls of this can safely be taken daily, and in severe cases people with strong constitutions can easily take 8 and sometimes 10 spoonfuls, as necessary. However, one should never take it in large quantities on the first day.

Stomach bitters to whet the appetite
1 part peppermint
3 parts cinnamon
10 parts gentian
10 parts sweet flag
10 parts bog-bean
20 parts absynth
20 parts centaury
20 parts orange rind
300 parts brandy

Leave to soak for a few days, filter and, if you like, sweeten to taste. Take 25–50 drops before a meal.

Stomach-strengthening tincture

15 gram (½ oz) blessed thistle
15 gram (½ oz) centaury
15 gram (½ oz) gentian
15 gm (½ oz) orange rind
4 tsp avens
12 gm (⅓ oz) wormwood
12 gm (⅓ oz) sweet flag root
1 litre (2 pints) brandy

Pour brandy over the herbs and leave the drink, well-covered, to stand for 14 days. Then filter and for those with a sweet tooth add sugar to taste. One can take 2 spoonfuls of this tincture before meals.

For stomach cramps

50 gm (1¾ oz) candied orange peel
20 gm (¾ oz) ordinary orange peel
60 gm (2 oz) sweet flag root, chopped
10 gm (⅓ oz) gentian root, chopped
2½ tsp centaury, the top sprigs
1 litre (2 pints) brandy

Let this stand for 14 days, filter and bottle. Take a spoonful several times when you have cramp in the stomach.

Flatulence and milk-stimulating elixir

15 gm (½ oz) aniseed
15 gm (½ oz) caraway
15 gm (½ oz) coriander
15 gm (½ oz) fennel
15 gm (½ oz) angelica
1 litre (2 pints) brandy

Let the herbs soak in the brandy for 14 days. Then filter and sweeten (optional).

Aromatic tincture for the wind and stomach-strengthening

50 gm (1¾ oz) cinnamon
20 gm (¾ oz) ginger
2½ tsp galangal root
2½ tsp cloves
2½ tsp cardamom
1 litre (2 pints) brandy

Put the herbs, covered with brandy, in a securely closed bottle, for 14 days. Then filter and take 15–20 drops of it as needed.

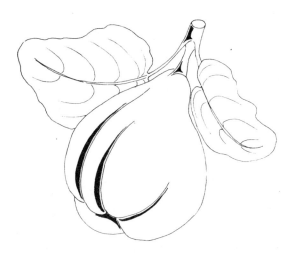

Quince liqueur is excellent for coughing and hoarseness, it loosens the phlegm. For the recipe see under *Ratafias and Fruits in alcohol*.

Sage Tincture for night sweat of people who suffer from consumption

100 gm (3½ oz) sage leaves, cut up
1 litre (2 pints) vodka

Filter after 8 days of soaking and sweeten if necessary. Take 20 to 30 drops 3 to 4 times a day. Recommended by the Russian physician Baimakoff.

Gold water for a long life

1½ tsp cinnamon
¾ tsp cloves
¾ tsp mace
rind of 1 lemon
3½ tsp coriander
10 gm (⅓ oz) orange blossom
2 leaves gold-leaf
1 litre (2 pints) eau de vie

Let the herbs soak in the eau de vie for 6 weeks. Then filter the drink and add 350 gm (¾ lb) of sugar. Cut the gold-leaf into tiny pieces and add to the liqueur.

Silver water for a slightly less prolonged life

3½ tsp angelica root
3½ tsp bitter almonds
10 gm (⅓ oz) rose petals
rind of 1 orange
1 litre (2 pints) eau de vie

Follow the same recipe as for Gold water.

Rosehip liqueur

Rosehip liqueur has a stimulating and strength-ening effect on old folk and is good for the most varied illnesses of the waterworks. For the recipe see under *Ratafias and Fruits in Alcohol*.

Garus elixir

2½ tsp myrrh (tincture)
1½ tsp cinnamon
¾ oz nutmeg
¾ oz cloves
½ oz aloe
1½ oz saffron
0.5 litre (1 pint) rectified spirit

Add all the ingredients together and leave to soak for at least 14 days. Then filter and add sugar syrup to taste as well as 1 spoonful of orange blossom water.

Spanish stomach consolation

3½ tsp aniseed
a pinch of cinnamon
a few cloves
a little nutmeg
a few walnuts
rind of ½ lemon
a little marjoram
a little chamomile
a little sage
a little lemon balm
1 litre brandy

Stir everything together, and leave for 40 days. Filter and add 250 gm (½ lb) of sugar.

Anti-hysteria liqueur

Take the seeds of wild parsnips, betony and lovage roots, 60 gm (2 oz) of each. Root of the single flower peony 125 gm (4 oz); mistletoe from the oak 90 gm (3 oz); myrrh 7 gm (¼ oz) and castor 14 gm (½ oz). Beat together well and add 125 gm (4 oz) of dried centipedes. Pour over 12 litre (24 pints) extract of mugwort (*artemisia vulgaris*) in water and 9 litres (18 pints) of brandy. Leave in a closed barrel for 8 days and distil in a closed, cold apparatus. Sweeten to taste.

Travel drops

Pour a good brandy over equal amounts of arnica flowers, centaury, wormwood and chamomile and filter after it has stood for 6 days. 10–15 drops on a lump of sugar or in water.

Unusual liqueurs and sundries

During my search for recipes I came across a lot of strange liqueurs. People have really tried all sorts of things, some of them quite absurd. Under the guise of miraculous properties spiders' heads, testicles and even a monkeys' foetus were added to liqueurs. I have tried a number of unusual liqueurs (none that were too ridiculous, but some of them very unlikely) and to my great surprise I even liked them. Not everyone will like these liqueurs, but some enterprising person might well find something to his liking among them, or feel the urge to start experimenting.

Strictly speaking, advokaat does not belong to the liqueurs, but it is so closely related that I have included recipes for this drink.

the inside of a vanilla pod
or a packet of vanilla sugar
a glass of persico or marasquin (optional)

Beat the yolks with sugar, salt and vanilla, until frothy. Continue beating and add the brandy. Warm, beating all the time, until it starts thickening, *au bain-marie* (*au bain-marie* means placing the pan with contents in another pan filled with boiling water, this is to prevent curdling.)

When the egg mixture is thickened, cool, still beating, and if you like add the persico or marasquin.

This advokaat can be kept for 1 to 2 weeks and in a securely closed, unopened bottle which is stored in a cool place, even up to a few months.

Advokaat I

20 gm egg yolks
400 gm (14 oz) sugar
1 litre (2 pints) brandy
a little salt and grated nutmeg

Advokaat II

Instead of 20 egg yolks use 20 eggs and 0.5 kilo (1 lb) of sugar. Then follow the recipe for Advokaat I. This drink keeps for a much shorter time, only a few days.

Advokaat *en procureur* can be made by putting a head of stiffly beaten, slightly sweetened egg white on top of the advokaat, and sprinkling some grated nutmeg over it.

Pumpkin liqueur

Take 0.75 kilo (1½ lb) of pumpkin (courgettes or zucchini), cut into small pieces, add the juice of one lemon and its rind, bring to the boil and simmer until done. Rub through a sieve or press through a cloth and add ¾ litre (1½ pints) of rum and 175 gm (6 oz) of sugar for each ½ litre (1 pint) of juice. Leave to soak for a few days. Filter and bottle.

Hanged man's pumpkin liqueur

Take a large pumpkin with a strong skin. Carefully slice off the top and spoon out the seeds. Fill the hollow with rum and brown sugar and close the pumpkin up again by sticking the top with sellotape. Hang the pumpkin in a net above the bowl. After a while—about three weeks—the juice will start leaking from the pumpkin. Then make a hole in the pumpkin and let the juice run into the bowl. Filter and bottle. You can also add a few pieces of orange rind to the rum, when putting it in the pumpkin.

Variation Follow the same method as above, but fill the hollow with brown sugar, previously activated yeast and the juice of 1 orange. When the juice starts leaking from the pumpkin, drain it into a bottle and cover closely with an airlock. Let the drink ferment.

When it has stopped fermenting, filter and add some rectified spirit to taste. Bottle.

Tomatoes in vodka

0.75 kilo (1½ lb) tomatoes
½ tsp caraway seed
1 tsp cloves
a stick of cinnamon
1 bottle vodka

Use nice firm tomatoes, skin them and cut them into small pieces. Put the tomato pieces in a preserving jar, add the herbs and pour over the vodka. Close the jar and after 14 days add sugar to taste. Wait another month before serving this drink.

Rice whisky

0.75 kilo (1½ lb) rice
250 gm (½ lb) raisins
0.75 kilo (1½ lb) sugar
juice of 2 lemons
2.5 litre (5 pints) warm water
15 gm yeast

Put the rice and the chopped raisins with the sugar, lemon juice and water in a large bowl. Add the yeast, which you have first dissolved in a little warm water. Let the mixture stand for 12 days, covered with a cloth. Stir occasionally for the first three days. Make sure it is in a warm place. Do not remove the froth until the final day, then filter the wine into an earthenware bottle or clean barrel. Leave in a cool place for 6 months. Bottle.

Pistachio liqueur

50 gm (1¾ oz) pistachio nuts
50 gm (1¾ oz) almonds
50 gm (1¾ oz) peach stones
rose essence
350 gm (¾ lb) sugar
1 litre (2 pints) eau de vie

Crush the nuts, almonds and kernels and let them soak in the eau de vie for a month. Filter the drink and add the sugar and rose essence. Bottle and leave to mature for another month.

Syrup Dutch gin

This is a traditional New Year's drink.

25 gm (1 oz) cinnamon sticks
0.5 kilo (1 lb) dark sugar cane syrup
1 litre (2 pints) Dutch gin, old

Put the cinnamon and an eggcup of Dutch gin in a saucepan, which should be well-covered. Bring to the boil and gently simmer for half an hour. Cool, add a little more Dutch gin and leave overnight, well-covered. Put the syrup in a pan with a lid.

Very carefully warm the syrup until it becomes fluid and keep adding Dutch gin, a little at a time, also the cinnamon-flavoured Dutch gin. Stir occasionally until everything is well mixed, but put the lid back on the pan each time. Bottle and leave to mature in a cool place.

Bishop's essence

30 gm (1¼ oz) bitter orange rind
a few cloves
1 stick cinnamon
1½ tsp nutmeg
1½ tsp ginger root
1½ tsp cardamom
1 litre (2 pints) brandy

Let all this soak for at least 3 weeks; filter and keep it until you want to drink Bishop's wine. Add one spoonful to a bottle of red wine and sugar to taste. Warm the drink and serve.

Liqueurs from Country Wines

Since distillation of both alcohol and of flavourings is illegal, and the price of spirits is prohibitive, making liqueurs at home requires a different approach to that used by commercial manufacturers. The English method of home liqueur making is based on the use of ingredients not previously discussed.

The first of these ingredients is homemade wine which, with an alcohol level of 16%, represents about a third of the total requirement of the finished drinks. The type of homemade wine that you use is not important providing that it does not possess and over-powering flavour that is going to contrast with that of the liqueur and that it has a fairly high alcohol level. Ideally use one that has the same flavour as the type of liqueur you plan to make. Do not use a wine that you do not like the taste of or one that is infected, for although the liqueur flavour will predominate and mask other tastes, if there is a strong 'off' flavour it will completely ruin the drink. *If you are in any doubt about a wine do not use it.*

Do not buy wines for liqueur making as often these are of lower alcohol content than their homemade equivalents and it would be almost as cheap to buy extra spirits and make the liqueurs by the methods given earlier.

Sugar Syrup and Glycerine

The type of liqueurs described above is designed for drinking immediately and this requires quick and effective mixing. It is also important to be able to make adjustments during the blending and this can only be achieved if a sugar syrup is used instead of solid sugar. The overall effect of using syrup and wine in place of spirits is that the drink is thinner than it should be. This can be overcome by adding glycerine which adds body and provides the drink with a degree of sweetness. Glycerine is naturally present in many wines and it is the amount in the drink that is one of the factors that determine the quality of some of the world's finest vintages. However, if you are against adding 'artificial chemicals' to your drink it is certainly not essential. If you do use it add at the rate of two tablespoons per litre.

A good way of avoiding excess dilution

when making the sugar syrup is by dissolving sugar in warm wine. Place the required amount of sugar in an enamelled or aluminium saucepan and cover with wine. Warm gently but do not bring to the boil as alcohol has a far lower boiling point than water and a large quantity of the spirit will be lost by evaporation. Dissolve all the sugar and gently stir the mixture to stop the sugar sticking to the bottom of the pan. Allow to cool and use the solution in the same way as sugar syrup. Sugar syrup should contain the maximum concentration of dissolved sugar possible in the water. A stock solution of sugar syrup containing one pound of sugar in a pint of water, or pro rata for smaller quantities is a good idea and this will keep for some time but it is adviseable not to make up too much, unless you know that you will be using it fairly quickly. Do not add solid sugar and hope that it will dissolve with time—it will but with the concentrations used it might take several months.

Essences and Flavourings

The third ingredient that you use in this method of liqueur production is artificial flavouring. These can be either essences sold specifically for the purpose or ordinary fruit flavourings. With flavourings sold specifically for the purpose the amount to add is given in the instructions, with fruit flavourings you will have to experiment to find the correct quantity. The essences are made by a variety of methods and the best ones use only the finest fruits and herbs, often employing a distillation technique based on a closely guarded formula like those of the great liqueur houses themselves. Many of the brands produce excellent results but few are better or offer a wider range of flavours than the T. Noirot range, available throughout the world or by post from the distributors 'Fermenta', Rolleston Road, Burton on Trent, Staffs, England.

The only equipment you will need is a 26 fluid ounce wine bottle or a one litre bottle. Some recipes using essences are designed for making a litre of drink and since adjusting the quantities to make any amount is easy the recipe table is based on making one litre of drink. If you wish to make a wine bottle full use only 70 per cent of the ingredients. Ideally use a bottle slightly larger than you require so that there is plenty of room to shake the liquid.

The container that you serve the liquid from is very important. Liqueurs whether bought or made suggest an elegant life style and it is important that the bottle lives up to this. Ideal for this purpose are the bottles used for a similar commercial liqueur which can be obtained from restaurants. You can of course, always serve them from a cut glass decanter. Ensure that you remove all traces of the label from the bottle as these soon become messy and wash the bottle thoroughly with soapy water to remove all stains.

Adjustments to the Drinks

When mixing liqueurs it is important to realise that with only very slight adjustments to the drink better results can be obtained. Liqueur blending is far easier than adjustments to wine or beer recipes since you get an instantaneous feed back as to the effect of changing any particular additive. Constant tasting, during all stages of manufacture will ensure that you arrive at the perfect product. Taste is everything and the world famous liqueurs were developed entirely this way with measurements being made only so that the taste could be reproduced accurately.

The order in which ingredients are placed in the mixing bottle might seem unimportant but a better mix is usually obtained by adding the spirit last. Place the essence, sugar syrup, wine and glycerine in the bottle and shake thoroughly. Although you will know the amount of spirit to add from the recipe table it is worthwhile only adding half initially and then tasting the result. Then add a half of what remains and again taste it, then add the rest of the spirit. In this way you will be able to judge for yourself the optimum quantity of the most expensive ingredient. You may decide that you can economise on the spirit or that the improved quality from further addition fully justifies the cost. In the same way you can adjust the sugar content but liqueurs are very sweet and it is unlikely that much advantage will be gained by increasing the sugar above the level quoted in the recipe. Additional wine will dilute the drink and whilst it might appear to represent a cheap way of increasing the volume it will be at the expense of quality.

Do not worry if the container is not full or that you leave a half empty bottle for any period of time. A liqueur is high in both sugar and alcohol and this combination produces an environment in which bacteria cannot survive. Therefore there is little chance of the drink becoming infected. This also seems to inhibit oxidation and, even when it does occur, the very strong flavouring of the essence masks it completely. Storage of liqueurs therefore presents very few problems.

These drinks can be served as soon as they have been thoroughly mixed, unlike those earlier in the book where it is necessary to leave standing for some time to ensure that the natural flavourings blend together. However it is still advisable to make the drink not less than three days and preferably about a fortnight before drinking.

Liqueur Recipes

Decide the type of spirit that you intend using and the required proof level of the finished drink (information on both of these can be found earlier in the book).

Since the only operation required is the mixing of the liquid ingredients there is no need to change from the general method. With full fruit drinks, especially those that contain brandy in their name it is best to use brandy to get the full deep flavouring. With light drinks such as mint based liqueurs vodka, the virtually flavourless spirit, should be employed. In place of vodka, Polish Spirit, which at 140 proof is twice as strong as vodka, can be used (of course only half the volume should be used). This ingredient is now, however, difficult to obtain.

Consult the chart to see the quantity of each liquid needed. You will see that in order to maintain the balance in the liqueur the quantity of sugar rises with the amount of spirit used, whilst at the same time the quantity of wine decreases. This allows for an infinite variation in the formulations that can be compounded for any one liqueur, although in some cases the essences may be slightly overpowering if you use too little spirit. If this is the case add only three quarters of the essence initially, taste and add more a drop at a time until you are satisfied. Using this technique and taking the amounts from the chart it is possible to make less alcoholic drinks cheaper than by any other means, as well as producing drinks virtually identical to the well known commercial brands.

Notes on the use and compilation of Table

The chart is based on the assumptions that:
1. the volume occupied by the wine and spirits is 27 fluid ounces (726ml), the remaining volume being occupied by sugar essences, glycerine and the air space necessary for shaking.
2. the percentage of alcohol in the wine is fifteen. The liqueur maker will not know the actual figure, but small variations will have an insignificant effect on the alcoholic strength.
3. the spirit strength is 65° proof British (the strength of most available spirits). Using slightly stronger spirits will hardly influence the final alcohol concentration and can usually be ignored. It will be necessary to dilute stronger spirits such as Polish spirit (preferably with wine) before using. A fifty per cent dilution of Polish spirit usually produces ideal results.
4. the sugar is diluted with wine. Use of water will again only slightly affect the alcohol level.

It must be stressed that it is the balance of the liqueur that is important and not the actual level of the alcohol present. Even if all the possible errors are compounded it will not result in a liqueur of noticeably lower quality.

DO NOT WORRY TOO MUCH ABOUT THE STRENGTH OF YOUR DRINK—IF IT TASTES RIGHT IT IS RIGHT. IF IT DOES NOT SEEM STRONG ENOUGH ADD SPIRIT UNTIL IT DOES.

Quantities of spirits, wines and solid sugar necessary to make various strength liqueurs

Volume of wine		Vol of spirits (65°)		Weight of sugar		Strength	
						In degrees proof	
Fl ounces	mls or ccs	Fl ounces	mls or ccs	Ounces	Grams	British	USA
33	924	0	0	2	56	25.5	29.2
28	784	4	112	4	112	29.3	34.9
23	644	8	224	11	308	33.0	37.7
18.5	418	11	308	9	252	35.0	40.6
14.5	406	14	392	11	308	37.9	43.3
11.5	322	16.5	462	11.5	322	40.4	46.1
8	224	19	532	12	336	42.5	48.5
5	140	23	644	12.5	350	47.8	54.6
3	84	24.5	686	13	364	49.1	56.0
0	0	27	726	14	392	51.6	59.0

Liqueur Flavoured Wines

This represents the halfway house between liqueur making and wine making and combines the taste and flavour of liqueur with the economy of wine.

The method employed consists of adding the flavouring to a gallon (4.5 litres) of fermenting wine must. The essence is greatly diluted, but the lower alcohol and sugar level of the wine will require far less flavouring to achieve a balance. In effect a dilute liqueur is obtained which can be drunk as it is or to which sugar syrup and brandy or vodka can be added to taste.

To make the wine liqueur you will require
1 lb (0.5 kilos) of sultanas
3 lb (1.5 kilos) sugar
2 level teaspoonfuls of citric acid
Wine yeast
1 gallon (4.5 litres) water
one container of liqueur essence

Mince the sultanas and place together with the sugar and citric acid in a plastic bucket. Cover with six pints (3 litres) of boiling water. Cover the bucket and allow the temperature to drop to 65°–70°F (18–21°C), then add the yeast. Maintain this temperature throughout the fermentation. Stir daily and allow the vigorous head to develop. When the head has subsided, usually between five and ten days, strain the liquid into a demijohn, add the liqueur essence and top up to the gallon with tap water. Fit an airlock. Rack after the first

heavy sediment has formed (the time that this takes will depend upon the temperature at which the fermentation has taken place, but will usually be between two and four months). When the wine has cleared it will be ready for either drinking or fortifying and sweetening, or using as the base wine for making liqueurs by the process discussed above.

Mock Spirits

Today it is possible to be completely self sufficient in all alcoholic drinks with the exception of spirits. It had long been considered that the only way to overcome this problem was to use an illegal still. Quite apart from the legal aspects this presents many problems. First it would be necessary to produce the alcoholic brew to be distilled, not a difficult problem, but nevertheless a stage at which errors can be introduced which would be magnified in the distillation. It is the distillation itself which presents the almost insurmountable problem. Not only would you have to design the still, but you would have to operate it correctly. Simply scaling down a commercial still and adapting the professional stills, even if you have access to them, will not guarantee success. Unlike beer making where the worst that can result is a bad tasting beer, if the still is not operated correctly then toxins such as wood alcohol will be concentrated to a level at which they could have very harmful effects on anyone drinking them over a prolonged period. Although the authors of novels and plays would have us believe that in certain parts of the world illegal distillation is almost a cottage industry, with skills passed from father to son, by its very nature nothing is known on the long term health effects that it has on the drinkers.

It became obvious that if the spirit drinker was to enjoy the same amount of freedom as the wine and beer drinker, a method of making mock spirits had to be found. This is limiting as the maximum alcohol concentration that can normally be obtained by fermentation is about sixteen per cent whereas most spirits sold are much higher than this. Most spirits however are diluted with water, tonic or a variety of mixers and when consumed the true alcohol level is roughly the same as can be made by fermentation alone. This gave a method of producing a drink similar to that normally found in the glass rather than the bottle. The method given below is for an imitation spirit, it should never be thought of as a true spirit and should not be used in any of the preceding recipes for liqueur making. It is at its best drunk straight, without additives, although you can always experiment and add tonic or another mixer if you wish, and you can always have two glasses instead of one if you find it too weak.

Whiskora, Ginora, and Brandora are all marketed by Southern Vineyards, Hove, Sussex, England and are mock spirits produced by fermentation. The secret of these concentrates lies in the essence which retains its

spirit type flavour throughout the fermentation. By adding one bottle of either whisky, gin or brandy to the finished product the drink bears a remarkably strong resemblence to the true spirit at only a fraction of the price of the real thing. Many spirit drinkers have taken to these and it is sold world wide, but if you take your spirits neat or are a connoisseur then you are unlikely to be satisfied with this substitute. But the vast majority of tipplers will find these mock spirits as agreeable to their palates as they are to their pockets.

To make the drinks, which come complete with instructions, requires winemaking techniques which are fully described in *Winemaking Month by Month* but for the benefit of those who do not usually make their own wine the general method is very simple.

The only equipment required is a demijohn, an airlock and preferably a wine filter such as a Vinbrite—all of which can be obtained from the same supplier as the concentrate. As with all home produced drinks it is essential to ensure that all the equipment is thoroughly sterilised before use. Failure to do this could result in an undrinkable, infected drink. The quickest and most efficient method of sterilisation is to stand the equipment for ten minutes in a solution of one pint (0.5 litre) of water to which one tablespoonful of domestic bleach has been added. Bleach is extremely poisonous and it is essential to ensure that not only the equipment is thoroughly washed after use, but that the fumes are not breathed in. Obviously this sterilising solution should not be allowed to come into contact with either the concentrate or the drink during any stage of the preparation. If you observe these precautions you will not have any difficulties.

Pour the concentrate into the demijohn and wash out the container with warm water to ensure that it has all been transferred. Then dissolve 1 lb 5 oz (600 gm) of household sugar into a container full of warm water and transfer to the demijohn. This sugar will provide much of the alcohol of the drink but do not be tempted to add further alcohol to increase the strength as the liquid has been carefully balanced to produce the best results without any problems of stuck ferments. Top up the demijohn, leaving about one pint (half a litre) air space and add a wine yeast such as Vinkwik. Maintain the temperature at 77°F (25°C) if possible. Failing this, providing the temperature does not drop below about 65°F (18°C) the fermentation will occur, but it will take far longer. Do not be tempted to conduct the operation above 77°F as off flavours may develop.

Within two days fermentation will be seen to start, allow the head to develop but as soon as it subsides, fill the demijohn with water to within an inch (2.5 cm) of the airlock. Failure to do this may result in the drink having an oxidised flavour, which can upset the delicate balance. Maintain the temperature given above until fermentation ceases. This can be checked by an hydrometer where a reading of 1.000 or below means that all of the available sugar has been converted into alcohol. If you do not have an hydrometer you can check that the liquid has finished working by periodically examining the airlock, when bubbles cease to escape this stage in the operation is complete.

When fermentation has finished, add four Campden tablets and two stabiliser tablets, both available from the same source as the concentrate, and leave for a week in order that the yeast may settle at the bottom of the container. Here the technique differs from that usually employed in winemaking. In winemaking it is usual to rack, add Campden tablets and top up with water to stop oxidation. Since a high alcohol level is essential with mock spirits, water must not be added at this stage. Few people would be prepared to add expensive spirits to a drink that is not clear and therefore it is advisable to filter the drink through a wine filter which although costing about as much as a bottle of Scotch but once bought can be used for any number of brews.

Rack the liquid by syphoning and then filter. You will find that due to the loss of the deposit at the bottom of the container you will have less than a gallon of liquid. Taste the liquid and whilst it is recommended that you add a bottle of spirit to the gallon, it is advisable to first add half a bottle to ascertain its effect. Then check again after adding the full bottle. In this way it is possible to determine the minimum quantity of bought spirit that it is necessary to provide.

Blending is very much a personal thing and

you may feel that you would prefer to add more than the recommended quantity. Of course this will make the drink more expensive but it will still be much cheaper than buying the equivalent volume of spirit.

Irish Whiskey

No book on the world's great drinks would be complete without a mention of Irish coffee. Although this is not technically a liqueur it is in the only sense that matters—the taste. Take a cup and two thirds fill it with hot strong black coffee, then add three teaspoonfuls of demerara sugar and about one and a half fluid ounces of Irish Whiskey. Stir until the sugar has dissolved. Pour double cream slowly on to the back of a spoon just touching the top of the coffee. The cream should then float on the top of the coffee. Drink the hot coffee through the cream which should be consumed towards the end.

These variations on the liqueur making process that have evolved recently mean that we can now increase the variety of drinks that we can make and enjoy to include virtually all of the worlds famous drinks. As well as saving money by these methods it has the advantage of the sense of achievement, something which you can never buy however large your cheque book.

Brian Leverett

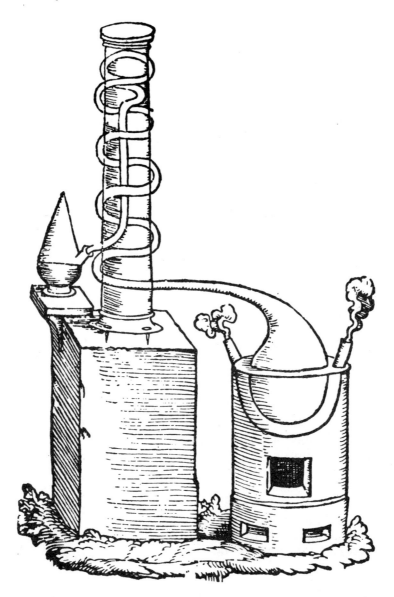

In conclusion

In his book *On Drink*, Kingsley Amis says that liqueur gives a bad hangover, but this is not so much a result of the drink itself, but more of its combination with the drinks that usually precede it. However, should you unexpectedly have too much to drink, then drink a large amount of water before going to bed and take an aspirin or stomach powder with it. It really helps, but you have to be capable of remembering to do it!

Unfortunately in many countries it is against the law to distil your own drinks and in England it is enough to be caught with a condenser, that spiral shaped tube, so important for home distillation. The following joke demonstrates this:

A man had to appear before the judge because he was accused of distilling without a licence.

'Where is the proof of this charge?' roared the judge.

'This, your honour, was found on his premises,' answered the prosecutor. And he pointed to evidence A, undeniably a condenser.

'Case proven,' said the judge. 'Does the accused have anything to add?'

'Yes, your honour. I would also like to plead guilty to rape.'

'You would like to do what?' exclaimed the surprised judge.

'If it please your honour. Although I have the tools for both, I did not do either.'

INDEX

Making Your Own Paté

Joyce Van Doorn

Pâté is a savoury mixture of meat, poultry, pulses or fish, sometimes covered with a pastry crust. This book mostly consists of mouth-watering recipes from around the world including dishes not normally described as pâtés in Great Britain such as terrines, mousses, gallantines, rillets, pies and flans.

Author

Joyce van Doorn is a lecturer, writer and broadcaster.

8″ x 8″, 120 pages
Full colour photographic cover
25 line drawings
ISBN 0 907061 01 X   Hardback £5.95
ISBN 0 907061 02 8   Paperback £2.95

Making Your Own Preserves

Jane & Rob Avery

A comprehensive book of over 150 recipes with careful instructions and all the essential background.

Contents

Authors

Rob and Jane Avery are freelance writers specialising in fishing, self-sufficiency and cookery topics.

8″ x 8″, 120 pages
Full colour photographic cover
Numerous line drawings
ISBN 0 907061 17 6   Hardback £6.95
ISBN 0 907061 18 4   Paperback £2.95

The Bread Book

Debbie Boater

A very basic book with fundamental information about the important role that bread plays in our diet and how to make it in its original, nutritious, wholesome form. A wide variety of recipes are included which cover breads, savoury breads, sweet breads, flat breads, pancakes, muffins and pastries.

Author

Debbie Boater is a teacher and founder of the Wholefood School of Nutrition.

8″ x 8″, 96 pages
Full photographic cover
25 line drawings
ISBN 0 904727 95 5   Hardback £5.95
ISBN 0 904727 96 3   Paperback £2.95

Bean Cuisine

Janet Horsley

Bean Cuisine is a comprehensive guide to the cooking of beans and pulses, useful both as a reference book and as a recipe book.

An introductory chapter traces the historic, economic and nutritional aspects of bean cooking, and explains how to use them to make well balanced, nutritious meals. An illustrated A-Z is included to aid recognition, as well as all the information needed to prepare, cook, freeze and sprout the beans.

Author

Janet Horsley is a cookery and nutrition lecturer.

8″ x 8″ 96 pages
Illustrated with line drawings
Full colour photographic cover
ISBN 0 907061 32 X   Hardback £6.95
ISBN 0 907061 33 8   Paperback £2.95

Making Your Own Liqueurs

Joyce van Doorn

With the help of some simple equipment: a set of scales, glassware, a filter and a mixture of herbs, spices, flowers, fruits, sugar and alcohol, you can make your own liqueurs which will be as exotic and tasty as the commercial varieties. Over 200 different recipes are listed ranging from fruits in alcohol, ratafias, herb and flower liqueurs, to bitters and elixirs.

Author

Joyce van Doorn is a lecturer, writer and broadcaster.

8″ x 8 ″, 120 pages
Full colour photographic cover
65 line drawings
ISBN 0 907061 03 6   Hardback £5.95
ISBN 0 907061 04 4   Paperback £2.95

Tea

Eelco Hesse

Tea drinking originated in China and Japan more than 2000 years ago. This book recounts the fascinating history of tea drinking and the colourful development of the Tea Trade over the centuries.

The author also examines the tools of tea making and how tea is grown and processed throughout the world. There is a section on tea blending and full instructions on making a 'perfect cup of tea'. The appendices contain anecdotes, songs and poetry about tea as well as useful addresses for further information and obtaining supplies.

Author

Eelco Hesse is a well-known authority on tea and the tea trade.

8" x 8", 120 pages
Full colour photographic cover
Numerous line drawings and engravings
ISBN 0 907061 05 2   Hardback   £6.95
ISBN 0 907061 06 0   Paperback   £2.95

Winemaking Month by Month

Brian Leverett

"If you enjoy making wines as well as drinking them you wil find this book both informative and enjoyable. It gives recipes for each month, according to what is in season as well as general guidance on home brewing"
Birmingham Post
"Useful, readable and logically presented."
Do-It-Yourself Magazine

Author

Brian Leverett is a lecturer, journalist and broadcaster.

8″ x 8″, 120 pages
Full colour photographic cover
37 line drawings and tables
ISBN 0 904727 93 9   Hardback £5.95
ISBN 0 904727 94 7   Paperback £2.95

Home Beermaking

Brian Leverett

This book is more than just a collection of recipes with instructions. It explains clearly, with straightforward diagrams, the complex brewing process and how to achieve the best possible results at home, whether from a can or with the traditional ingredients. The unique fault finder chart will help you overcome many of the problems that you may have had with previous attempts at home brewing.

Author

Brian Leverett is a lecturer, journalist and broadcaster.

8″ X 8″, 120 pages
Full colour photographic cover
32 line drawings and tables
ISBN 0 907061 07 9 Hardback £5.95
ISBN 0 907061 08 7   Paperback £2.95